FORTY ACRES

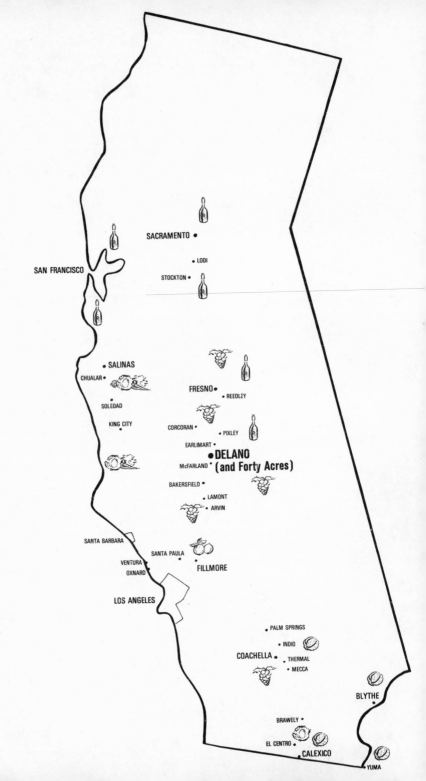

Forty Acres

Cesar Chavez and the Farm Workers

Mark Day

INTRODUCTION BY
CESAR CHAVEZ

PRAEGER PUBLISHERS
New York · Washington · London

Acknowledgments: I am grateful to the staff and parishioners of Our Lady of Guadalupe Church, Delano, to Fathers Al Peck, Ed Fronske, Ignatius DeGroot, Dave Duran, and Tom Messner, and to Ray Reyes and Lala Granillo for their many kindnesses. I am also indebted to the staff of *El Malcriado*—Doug Adair, Marcia Sanchez, Ben Madocks, and Richard Ibarra. My special thanks to Andy Zermeno, a sensitive man and a talented artist. I also owe thanks to: Dorothy Day and the *Catholic Worker* for permission to adapt for use in this book my first article, "A Steak Dinner or a Plate of Beans?"; Bob Hoyt, editor of *The National Catholic Reporter,* for permission to use material from my article "The Grape Boycott: Where Is It Now?" (copyright April 24, 1970, *The National Catholic Reporter*); Clay Barbeau, editor of *Way Magazine,* for permission to adapt "The Black Eagle and the Grapes of the Desert"; the Delano Historical Society; Ken Blum; writer Jacques Levy; five diligent journalists: Ron Taylor, of the *Fresno Bee,* Bill Acres, formerly of the *Delano Record,* Helen Manning and Eric Brazil, of the *Salinas Californian,* and Sam Kushner, of the *People's World*; Bob Thurber, Gene Daniels, Stanley Randal, George Ballis, Chris Sanchez, Bob Fitch, and Gerald Sherry, editor of the *Central California Register,* for their memorable photographs; the *Fresno Bee*; the *Delano Record*; and Juan A. Cuauhtemoc for his poem "*Ese Chuy, Jesus,*" from *Poesias de la Causa.* Finally, my thanks to Mike Kratko, cowpuncher, farm worker, and maintenance man of Forty Acres, who kept us all in stitches during those gloomier days! I am pleased to name all these people who helped my book. Some other names of people who appear in the narrative have been changed at the author's discretion. Many thanks to Robert Montoya for the map and to Andy Zermeno for his drawings on pages 24 and 52.

TO
MY PARENTS,
TO ALAN MC COY AND MY OTHER FRANCISCAN CONFRERES
FOR STANDING BY ME THROUGH DIFFICULT TIMES,
AND TO MY BROTHERS AND SISTERS, THE FARM WORKERS,
THAT THEY MAY CONTINUE TO GAIN
A MORE ABUNDANT SHARE
IN THE HARVEST
OF THEIR
ENDLESS
TOIL

Contents

8   *Contents*

A SECTION OF ILLUSTRATIONS FOLLOWS PAGE 128.

Introduction

BY CESAR CHAVEZ

A great deal of change has taken place among farm workers since our struggle began in 1965. Before the strike started, we had to work ten days in order to get ten people together for a meeting. Now we can get a thousand people to a meeting in only a few hours. The awareness of the people has been magnified a thousand times over. People have lost their fear. And, because there has been a concrete success in Delano, workers throughout the country are making fantastic demands on our time, organizers, and resources. If we had the resources, we could be organizing simultaneously all over the southwestern United States.

I have always believed that, in order for any movement to be lasting, it must be built on the people. They must be the ones involved in forming it, and they must be the ones that ultimately control it. It is harder that way, but the benefits are more meaningful and lasting when won in this fashion. It is necessary to build a power base. Money by itself does not get the job done. This is why poverty programs have so much difficulty. Although many nice things are said and many wheels are spinning, very little real social change takes place. To try to change conditions without power is like trying to move a car without gasoline. If the workers are going to do anything, they need their own power. They need to involve themselves in meaningful ways. Once they achieve a victory, they can make use of their power to negotiate and change things for the better.

I have often been asked what kind of a union I am trying to build and what type of society I want to see in the future. It seems to me that, once the union members are taken care of in terms of better wages and working conditions, the union must involve itself in the major issues of the times. The problem often arises that a group gets too involved in its own successes and doesn't have time for anything else. It is my hope that we keep ourselves focused on our ideals. It is much easier to profess something by words and not by deeds. Our job, then, is to educate our members so that they will be conscious of the needs of others less fortunate than themselves. The scope of the worker's interest must motivate him to reach out and help others. If we can get across the idea of participating in other causes, then we have real education.

As for the nation as a whole, it doesn't matter to me how our government is structured or what type of political party one may have. The real change comes about when men really want it. In a small way we try to change ourselves and we try to change those with whom we come into contact. You can't organize the masses unless you organize individuals. I like to think of our group as a "doer" type union. We place a great deal of emphasis on doing things and very little on theorizing or writing about them.

I think that our philosophy of cooperation with all groups has helped us a great deal. Our people have developed the ability to respect everyone with whom they come into contact: a wealthy church group or a poor Puerto Rican group in New York City. We try to respect their beliefs and ideals. We try to get them to help us on their own terms. We attempt to show them that by assisting us they are doing something to solve their own problems. A lot has to do with respecting other groups. The best thing we have going for us is having all kinds of people help us in a variety of ways.

For example, we tell people, "If you don't eat lettuce today, you are really helping us." This is the key to successful organizing: letting people who want to help know what they can do. Many movements do not reach this stage. Everything we do must be clearly defined.

During the course of our struggle, we have come to realize that the poor and disadvantaged will not make the gains they need only by political action. We must do more than merely involve ourselves in politics. A grape grower in Delano has one vote. We have a thousand votes to his one vote. But the grower can pick up a telephone, call Washington, and make himself heard. He has more power than we do. We have begun to ask *why*. Obviously, he has more power because he has the economic power. If we had economic power, our thousand votes would count a thousand times more than any individual's vote.

Economic development is a *must* for our membership. Why can't farm workers have a bank? Their wages will still be low for many years to come. If we can retain our increases by buying cooperatively, I think we will be in good shape. We must also get away from the "superconsumerism" atmosphere that surrounds us. We are virtually forced to buy everything that glitters and shines.

Meanwhile, I am not so alienated as others about the absence of political leadership here in the United States. We felt the loss of John and Robert Kennedy very keenly. But, despite this present bad season, I am confident that leadership will appear that is responsive to the needs of the people. Bad times bring good times!

I am often asked if our youth, especially the young Mexican Americans, will choose the way of violence to make the necessary changes in our society. I don't think that violence will be a way of life for any significant number of people. Although many may espouse the rhetoric of violence, few will physically commit violence. Meanwhile, we must be vitally concerned about educating people to the significance of peace and nonviolence as positive forces in our society. But our concern must not be frozen on a highly sophisticated level. We are concerned with peace, because violence (and war is the worst type of violence) has no place in our society or in our world, and it must be eradicated. Next to union contracts, we must focus our attention to bring about the necessary changes in our society through nonviolent means. We must train effective organizers for this purpose.

We must acquaint people with peace—not because capitalism is better or communism is better, but because, as men, we are better. As men we don't want to kill anyone, and we don't want to be killed ourselves. We must reach everyone so that this message can go out. If we do this correctly, our people will rise above mere material interests and goals. They will become involved in cultural matters. And we need a cultural revolution among ourselves—not only in art but also in the realm of the spirit. As poor people and immigrants, all of us have brought to this country some very important things of the spirit. But too often they are choked, they are not allowed to flourish in our society.

People are not going to turn back now. The poor are on the march: black, brown, red, everyone, whites included. We are now in the midst of the biggest revolution this country has ever known. It really doesn't matter, in the final analysis, how powerful we are, how many boycotts we win, how many growers we sign up, or how much political clout we possess, if in the process we forget whom we are serving. We must never forget that the human element is the most important thing we have—if we get away from this, we are certain to fail.

This book, by Father Mark Day, tells of our struggle.

It is unique, inasmuch as it was written by an insider, and it is my hope that it will attract more followers to our cause.

CESAR E. CHAVEZ
Director,
United Farm Workers Organizing
Committee, AFL-CIO
Delano, California

October 12, 1970

Joining the Struggle:
A Personal Prologue

After reading and hearing about the grape situation, all the
people I know wonder why you don't keep your nose in
your church and mind your own business.

If we want to buy grapes you will not tell us what to do.
Where do you buy your wine?

We use a church for peace, not to stir up more problems.
Keep your nose out of other people's way of making an
honest living.—an anonymous letter

My first contact with farm workers in the San Joaquin
Valley was in the Stockton area. I was sent there with
five of my classmates after our ordination into the priesthood in 1965. Stockton, a lusty farm town and inland
port, was a far cry from seminary life in Santa Barbara,
with its mountains, beaches, and middle-class resort atmosphere (this was before the oil slick and bank-burning). I
welcomed the change. Santa Barbara spoke of a Franciscan
response from the past. In Stockton, I was forced to deal

with real problems and with people who were the victims of society.

My classmates and I heard lectures on pastoral counseling and took turns as chaplains in the hospitals and jails during our year in Stockton. My own interests centered on the farm workers. Thousands of them—Filipinos, Mexicans, Mexican Americans, and blacks—lived in our parish. It was not difficult to see that their plight was mainly economic. Part of the parish embraced the "Islands"—the rich farm land along the San Joaquin River Delta, where potatoes, tomatoes, and asparagus are grown on the corporation farms.

Economic oppression, racism, and the powerlessness of the farm worker became immediately evident. Our church, St. Mary's, is situated in the heart of Stockton's skid row. Only a few blocks away was the "shape up," where farm workers were recruited by farm-labor contractors and herded onto buses like animals in the wee hours of the morning. The strong were taken. The weak were left behind.

I was once invited to attend a three-day conference on farm workers at the University of California at Davis. The fact that no farm workers were in attendance disturbed me, so I borrowed a Volkswagen bus and transported ten field hands from the "shape up" to the conference. The public-health nurses and state-salaried people were aghast when I brought the men into the seminars and workshops. The workers spoke persuasively, but the whole affair convinced me that nobody really cared about, or wanted to listen to, the farm worker.

Many of the workers came from Mexico and were exploited both on the job and by the merchants in the town. The workers desperately needed some power of their own. Government handouts and War on Poverty programs were demoralizing and divisive. They only served to enrich a few, salve the consciences of others, and, in general, keep the rich and the poor in their respective places.

Father Alan McCoy, pastor of St. Mary's at that time, was well known for his work among the people. He had started a credit union and a soup kitchen and had organized a variety of self-help projects for low-income people. His strong objections to the infamous *bracero* program (the importation of single men from Mexico) had set him at odds with farmers in the area. His encouragement has meant much to me to this day.

There had been several attempts to organize farm workers in the Stockton area. All of them had run into serious difficulties, partly because of the strength and terrorism of the farmers and partly because of the inadequate methods used by the organizers. The most recent attempts had been aided by two Catholic priests: Fathers Donald McDonnell and Thomas McCullough. They were partially responsible for founding the Agricultural Workers Organizing Committee, AFL-CIO. Al Green and Norman Smith were two of the guiding lights in the organization. The union made some gains but never really got off the ground.

In my naïveté, I made several attempts to hold meetings with farm-labor contractors and growers in order to alleviate some of the worst problems. But at best all they wanted to do was talk. They had absolutely no desire to improve the lot of workers. I became convinced that what had happened in Delano had to be repeated in Stockton. But the question was—When?

I was quite familiar with the Chavez movement through the coverage it had received in the mass media. I later learned that Cesar Chavez was born in Yuma, Arizona, and raised in the migratory farm-labor stream that runs between Arizona and California. He had lived in the Imperial Valley, in Delano, and also in the San Jose area of California. His formal education was limited, and, after he did a stretch in the Navy, he returned to San Jose and did some sharecropping with his brother Richard.

Cesar and his family often joke about his former flair for playing expert pool and dressing sharply. But there was no joke about the abject poverty and powerlessness that he and his fellow Chicanos felt in the barrios.

Cesar was a close friend of Father Don McDonnell's when the latter served as a young parish priest in the East San Jose area. McDonnell showed a deep interest in the economic plight of the barrio-dwellers. The young priest was notable in that he lived poorly and communicated fluently in Spanish with his parishioners. He also knew a great deal about farm-labor history, and Cesar often mentions that the priest taught him about the church's social teachings on the rights of the working man.

When Fred Ross arrived in the barrio in San Jose, Cesar and his friends thought he was just another phony social worker or do-gooder. But the tall, lanky, soft-spoken organizer manifested none of the condescension or the other negative attributes associated with community workers. Ross had been assigned by Saul Alinsky, of the Industrial Areas Foundation, to train organizers for the Community Service Organization (CSO), a kind of NAACP for the Chicanos.

Cesar, responding rapidly to Ross's ideas and suggestions, worked at a furious pace as an organizer. He soon became national president of the CSO, defeating a candidate who referred to him as a "bare-footed Indian." But Chavez became discouraged at the hesitant attitude the CSO had on the issue of farm labor. He knew that the bulk of California's poor Mexican Americans were exploited by agribusiness. He was determined to do something about it. He left the CSO and eventually founded the National Farm Workers Association. Dolores Huerta, Gilbert Padilla, and Tony Orendain, now United Farm Workers Organizing Committee (UFWOC) vice-presidents, were some of his early CSO associates.

In February, 1967, I passed through Delano and decided to stop and talk with Cesar Chavez. I was on my way to make a week's retreat at Mission San Antonio, near the coast. It was a typical damp and overcast winter day in the San Joaquin Valley. The vines, barren and recently pruned, looked like knotted crosses on the bleak horizon.

Cesar's office was called the "pink house" and was located near the corner of Asti and First streets, on the west side. A two-bedroom house had been converted into the executive offices of the fledgling union. As I waited, farm workers and college-age volunteers came and went in a bustle of excitement.

Cesar was in conference with his assistant director, Larry Itliong, and with Dolores Huerta. I was invited into a small cubicle whose walls were decorated, fittingly, with a picture of *La Virgen de Guadalupe* and two of Mexico's revolutionary heroes, Padre Miguel Hidalgo and Emiliano Zapata. Cesar shook my hand warmly, smiled, and asked to be pardoned for the delay. His smile revealed a congenial attitude, as well as two gold fillings in his front teeth. When he spoke, he dramatized his feelings with several different facial expressions. When he told of the lack of local church support for the strike, he took on an air of helpless bewilderment, looking up to the ceiling in desperation. When he spoke of the need for a strong union and a tough boycott, he gritted his teeth and hit his fist on the table. But he remained calm and soft-spoken throughout. As he spoke, he habitually brushed a shock of black hair back from his forehead.

I was flattered when he said that he had received good reports on my work in Stockton. He told me that priests sympathetic to the cause were badly needed in Delano. I assured him that I would try to get permission to work in the Fresno diocese, which extends southward to Tulare and Kern counties.

I carried a very positive impression with me as I left

Delano. Cesar and his staff workers were selfless, hard-
working, and dedicated people. There was happily no
evidence of the petty bureaucracy one finds in War on
Poverty offices. Nor was there any deadening fear that the
establishment was under fire. This was taken for granted.
The small group of organizers was busy fighting a life-
and-death struggle for the survival of the union. I could
easily identify with the entire situation.

Father Alan McCoy was named superior of all the
Franciscans in the western United States shortly thereafter. With his help, I was assigned to do pastoral work
among the Spanish-speaking farm workers throughout the
Fresno diocese. I became involved with Cesar and his
union during the summer of 1967, just after the strike
against the Giumarra Vineyards Corporation began. As
one might expect, I ran into stiff opposition from the
local clergy and from a former bishop of the diocese. I
was forced to leave Delano once, but I was determined
to return, and I did so when a new bishop was installed
three months later. The battles with the clergy eventually
subsided, but the hostility is still very much in evidence.
Sometimes I think that many of the clergy will continue
to fight the unionization of farm workers, even after the
growers sign contracts with Chavez.

I gradually came to know and have a high regard for
not only Cesar and his wife, Helen, and their family but
all the strikers as well. The strike community in Delano
has always been a family too. Even now, several years after
the strike began, the family relationship is still very
strong. I developed close friendships with many of the
strikers, listened to their problems, married their sons and
daughters, baptized their babies, and buried their dead.

Besides fulfilling my strictly pastoral duties, I walked
picket lines near the vineyards, organized boycott support,
and served for a time as an editor of the farm workers'
newspaper, *El Malcriado*.

The greater part of this book is a product of my experience with *la huelga* (the strike). I have attempted to write neither a comprehensive history of the strike nor an in-depth study of Cesar Chavez. Least of all can my book be considered the work of an impartial or detached observer. I was and I am very much biased in favor of the farm workers, and I would not hesitate to repeat my actions on their behalf.

Somehow, in spite of my own failures and disappointments, I became a part of a progressive movement that offers solid hope to this country and to the world. Should even one person become a part of this struggle after reading these pages, I will consider this book a huge success.

MARK DAY

Delano, California

FORTY ACRES

"Mexican-American farm workers refer
to the place as Cuarenta Acres."

The Spirit of Forty Acres

This poem, by an anonymous author, is very popular in Mexico.

POEMA DEL CAMPESINO MEXICANO

A POEM OF THE MEXICAN FARM WORKER

Mi padre . . .
no podia escribir un poema.
Pero determinado su camino,
Por un pino haci' alla
En linea recta y veraz.
Formo con arado,
Un surco,
A traves d la labor.

My father . . .
could never write a poem.
But when he lined up his plow,
with a pine tree on a distant hill,
he made a furrow,
straight as an arrow,
across the length of his
labor.

Mi padre . . .
no podia escribir muchas
palabras.
Pero a levantar la cosecha,
En el sol del verano,
Creo,
Un poema . . .
De la tierra.

My father . . .
could not write
very many words.
But when he brought in
his crop
in the heat of a summer afternoon,
he created
a poem . . . from the earth.

An enlarged copy of this poem hangs in the farm workers' office at Salinas.

[I]

Delano: From Garces to Forty Acres

Delano came into existence, for all practical purposes, on July 14, 1873. It was at that time that the Southern Pacific Railroad announced that passenger service to the north was to begin from the Delano station in Kern County. The town was named after Columbus Delano, the Secretary of the Interior under President Grant. Stagecoach service was still the only link southward. At that time, the terrain was tumbleweed and sagebrush to the west, and beautiful grasslands and wild flowers that reached some thirty miles to the eastern foothills of the Sierra Nevada.

Garces Highway now crosses Delano from east to west and leads to the foothills near the spot where Padre Francisco Garces, a Franciscan missionary and trail blazer, baptized an Indian boy on May 3, 1771. The spot was discovered in recent years by Cecil Dyar, a local historian.

Only a few Chinese railroad workers permanently settled in Delano. The early settlers were families from the Midwest who started wheat farms. French sheepherders also arrived, and Delano became a shipping point for sheep, wool, and wheat in the 1880's. Names like Villard and Borel are still common in Delano. The Valencias, one of the early Mexican *Californio* families, still reside in Delano.

Several Japanese also lived in Delano until the infamous relocation took place in 1942. Rose Honbo, a Japanese American, once stated, "The Buddhist Church was built in Delano in 1930. There were about forty families in the congregation. But to our sorrow, the church was burned down during World War II, while the Japanese were in the relocation centers." The Japanese had owned several businesses in Delano, and many had farms. Few of them returned after the war.

Delano, like many of California's towns, once thrived with gambling and prostitution. One old-timer remarked to me, "My father told me that, as far back as 1906, the town had fourteen saloons and one grocery store." The women were told that "ladies" stayed away from towns like Bakersfield and Delano. During World War I, the army closed down several of the brothels. Some of the town's most "respectable" families were involved in the vice trade. They rationalized their activities by citing the heavy population of single men (mostly farm hands) and stated that their daughters had to be protected from attack in the streets. The White House and the Paradise Café were two favorite hangouts. Their patrons were politically influential in the area. Long-time residents bitterly remark that these vice lords effectively prevented industry and job opportunities from coming into the community.

In the early 1920's, cotton was introduced to the area. Blacks were brought from the South but found it difficult to compete with Mexican labor. Only a few hundred blacks now live in the area.

The first Filipinos to arrive began working at Joseph Di Giorgio's Sierra Vista ranch, east of Delano. Di Giorgio had just begun to grow grapes. The Filipinos were ideally suited to the agribusinessman's taste for profits, because they lived close together and cheaply in camps near the vineyards. They had been forbidden to marry under California's archaic and racist antimiscegenation laws.

During the early 1930's, the California Land Company (CLC) of Visalia, a holding company for the Bank of America, foreclosed on the Occidental Insurance Company and began to swallow up the small farms in the area. At one time, the CLC controlled 90 per cent of the farms in the area. The Filipinos were evidence of a new type of large-scale agriculture that needed cheap and plentiful labor.

The immigrants came from the Ilocos Islands under the servitude system. Their passage was paid by banks and rich families in the Philippines. The men had to pay back their fares as they worked in the vineyards—at 50 per cent interest. This required two to three years of hard labor for some of the men. "Many of them existed on a handful of rice and a few cents pay each day," a farmer told me.

The dust-bowl refugees from Oklahoma and other parts of the Midwest also arrived in the grape-growing areas of Kern and Tulare counties during the 1930's. "Delano and Earlimart [a nearby town] were in the heart of the *Grapes of Wrath* country," an old-timer told me. "People were so impoverished that they would undercut one another for a job. If a grower offered a man 25 cents an hour, another man would take the job for as little as 15 cents. Life was miserable, and people were starving." The dust-bowlers lived in Hooverville-type camps. Residents tell how the migrants would dismantle the old homesteaders' shacks in the foothills, in order to fuel their fires and keep warm.

Marin Caratan was one of the first Yugoslav settlers in the area. The Caratan family now controls the finest grape-producing land near Delano. Besides Caratan and Di Giorgio, names such as Perelli-Minetti, Wallace, Radovich, and Zaninovich became prominent in the area.

The Yugoslavs arrived in Delano in the late 1930's and early 1940's. Several factors, including hard work, cheap labor and land, and good prices, contributed to the rapid expansion of their farms. Nobody can deny the industriousness and many sacrifices that were essential ingredients of the success story of the Yugoslavs. Many had previously settled in other coastal cities from San Diego to Seattle, pursuing the trades of fishermen, longshoremen, and restaurant workers and owners. A few had tilled farms in other parts of the San Joaquin Valley.

Jack Zaninovich, a grape grower and a member of the Delano Historical Society, told me that conditions were favorable for a rapid expansion of the grape business in a relatively brief period of time. "Relatives made loans or the Slavs would borrow from other sources and buy land on a shoestring," he said. "Several Slavs like my uncle, Martin Gutunich, started in the restaurant business in Los Angeles and San Francisco. The land was very cheap and was bought on thirty-year terms at as little as 4 per cent interest. With only a little capital, one could develop a lot of acreage." Zaninovich added that the price of land fluctuates according to the demands of the market. "In 1922 through 1925, the land was worth almost $3,000 an acre. By 1929, it dropped to $150 an acre."

The growers made a killing on their grape crops. Some observers say that, although government marketing regulations dictated that grapes were to be sold for $2 a box, growers sold them for as high as $8 or $9 a box. The returns were put into new land, which was leveled and brought into production in a few years.

"We could hardly believe how they could expand so fast!" remarked Nick Yap, a Filipino and a long-time farm worker and striker with the United Farm Workers Organizing Committee (UFWOC). "Andy Zaninovich's farm grew from 160 acres to 2,000 acres, in *five* years."

The heaviest Mexican immigration to Delano occurred in the 1930's. The Mexicans came from Arizona, Texas, the Imperial Valley of California, and Mexico to work in the cotton fields. Many of them stayed only for a season, then worked their way northward. The families of Cesar Chavez and his wife, the former Helen Fabela, arrived in Delano during this period.

The migration of Mexicans and Mexican Americans has intensified since the 1930's. Grower spokesmen have stated, according to Richard Fineberg, that over 40 per cent of the harvest hands in the Delano area are "green-carders," or resident aliens from Mexico. Fineberg did a study on foreign agricultural labor in 1968. The unionization of farm workers has already decreased migrancy and has begun to stabilize the work force in the area.

During the summer of 1970, farm workers in the Delano area came to UFWOC's headquarters at Forty Acres by the thousands to sign with the union. Forty Acres is Delano's most recent landmark. It is located two miles west of Delano on Garces Highway, near the transmitting towers of the Voice of America. The late Walter Reuther once remarked that it was ironic that farm workers should struggle for a minimum of dignity in the shadows of the transmitters that told the *enslaved* peoples of the world about "the land of the free and the home of the brave."

The size of Forty Acres is insignificant when compared with the huge land holdings of the southern San Joaquin Valley. The average acreage of the vineyard corporations is 2,000 acres.

Mexican-American farm workers refer to the place as Cuarenta Acres. It is the place where Cesar Chavez fasted for twenty-five days in order to build a nonviolent base for his union. On one corner stand the executive offices of the farm union, dedicated to the memory of Roy Reuther, brother of the late United Auto Workers President. On another corner is a small newspaper office and a co-op service station. The newspaper is called *El Malcriado*. The gas station is made of adobe because Cesar Chavez loves the soil and the way the baked earth and dried mortar look in the hot valley sunlight. His brother Richard built the station and supervised the construction of a new administration building.

In a corner of the administration building is Cesar's office. In the late summer and early fall of 1970, the union leader spent much of his time elsewhere—in Los Angeles, Fresno, Bakersfield, and Salinas, negotiating and signing contracts with grape-, citrus-, melon-, and lettuce-growers. It was the season of the big breakthroughs. It was the time that the gentle yet intense man began to discover what five solid years of organizing could produce.

Chavez's office is simply decorated: a plain wooden table as a desk; a rocking chair for an aching back (the twenty-five-day fast had kept Cesar in bed for a year) ; a bookcase propped up by adobe bricks, supporting a bust of the late Senator Robert F. Kennedy and a framed picture of the late Martin Luther King, Jr. A smiling poster of Mahatma Gandhi all but covers one wall; the other is dominated by a picture of Our Lady of Guadalupe and a straw crucifix from Mexico. Near the door to Cesar's office are two large photographs: One shows Dorothy Day of New York's Catholic Worker; the other is that of the Berrigan brothers, Daniel and Philip, both priests who are now in prison for their denunciation of the war in Vietnam.

On one section of Forty Acres, Filipino strikers have begun a cooperative vegetable and cattle ranch. They plan to buy more land in order to build a pilot project of housing units—enough for forty or fifty men. If the project succeeds, it will be expanded to help thousands of elderly farm workers who have no community and nowhere to live when they retire.

In a far corner of Forty Acres, a large cross lies face down on the ground. Richard Chavez had made the cross from telephone poles. In the early spring of 1968, we decorated the fifteen-foot cross with roses and celebrated a sunrise Mass near it on Easter Sunday. Two days later, someone came during the night and cut down the cross, partially burning it with gasoline. It still lies there, bleached by two summers of sun, a reminder of the bigoted people who "don't like some Mexican telling us what to do."

Anglo volunteers, Mexicans, Filipinos, and lifelong farm workers work side by side without pay at Forty Acres in order to build an economic base for the rural poor. The scene provides a contrast to the city, which teems with small-minded merchants who have condemned the strike since its inception. The white lower middle class in Delano feels threatened by the rising expectations of the Chicano minority. A Veterans of Foreign Wars advertisement for a barbecue recently announced, "Come out on the 4th of July! Show that Delano has at least *some* Americans!"

A Mexican-American middle class has also emerged in the city's business community. These people encounter many difficulties and are pressured by the Anglo power structure to accommodate themselves to local prejudices. In order to succeed financially and socially, a few have become vociferous in their denunciations of Chavez and the strike. The young Chicanos refer to them as *Vendidos* (sellouts) or *Tio Tacos* (the Chicano version of Uncle Tom) .

Delano has come a long way from Padre Garces to Forty Acres. The grape strike has rescued the town from oblivion, but the scars of division and bitter polarization are still very much in evidence. It is my hope that some of the wounds that have been inflicted in Delano can be healed by creative thinking and dialogue among all segments of the community. Only this will combat the racism, fears, and petty hostilities that have run rampant in the city in recent years.

I am personally confident that Delano will prosper under the existing changes, brought about initially by the contracts between the grape growers and the union. It was in this hope and in this spirit that my book was written in the first place.

FORTY ACRES contains a glimpse of three years of my experience as a priest and volunteer with Cesar Chavez and his movement. The course of my life has been irrevocably changed. By sticking my nose into a small valley town in California's Central Valley, I have learned a great deal about what ails America and what can be done to fight oppression and racism everywhere. I have rubbed shoulders with Chavez and his followers, and I have come to regard many of them as the saints of a new era, men and women who have laid down their lives for a more human society and a new way of life for their brothers. And there is more to learn too.

[2]

Agriculture:
California's Most
Vital Revolution

The Council of California Growers frequently displays its motto on billboards and the pickup trucks that field foremen drive on the large farms: "Agriculture: California's Most Vital Industry." The phrase may be true or false. What cannot be disputed is that there is a revolution occurring within this $4.6-billion-a-year industry. This revolution is having far-reaching effects throughout the United States, where over 3 million farm workers have awakened to a now familiar battle cry: *Huelga!* (Strike).

Agriculture in California began around the early Franciscan missions that stretch from San Diego in the south to Sonoma in the north. A Jesuit missionary is credited with bringing the first vine cuttings to Baja California. From Baja, the vines were brought to upper California by the friars. San Gabriel Mission (near Los Angeles) became the principal wine-grape area in California.

When the mission lands were secularized, California was divided up into several large land grants. In his book *Factories in the Fields,* Carey McWilliams points out that large land grants were fraudulently acquired by a few landholders and speculators. Millions of acres were given to the railroads, and public officials were among those who unscrupulously grabbed all the land they could lay their hands on.

The structure of agriculture made it impossible for a small-family farmer to exist. Those who had intended to homestead and farm on a family basis were eventually forced to become laborers on the large spreads. Only the large, industrial-type farms survived. "The state was pervaded by a speculative, get-rich-quick psychology, which created the conditions suffered by agricultural labor today," states an article in *Manas* magazine (August 25, 1948).

The intensely individualistic and competitive nature of California agriculture has created a hostile climate for any cooperative schemes. Farm-labor unionization attempts have always been viewed as Trotskyite conspiracies.

In many areas of the state, an abundant supply of farm labor is necessary only from three to six months of the year. The agricultural industry and the state of California have never effectively come to grips with the seasonal unemployment of farm workers. If the present unenlightened "leadership" of men like Governor Ronald Reagan continues, these problems will undoubtedly be with us for many years to come.

The Chinese constituted the first supply of abundant cheap labor in California agriculture. They were mercilessly persecuted, and their further immigration was stopped by the Exclusion Act of 1882. The Japanese workers were militant and aggressive. They conducted several strikes and were eventually excluded under the gentleman's agreement of 1906. From 1920 onward, thousands of Mexicans and Filipinos were employed on California's farms. In 1929, dust-bowl refugees began to pour into California. Their chief entry point was Highway 66, which brought them through the town of Tehachapi into the San Joaquin Valley. Their sad plight was chronicled in the La Follette hearings and immortalized by John Steinbeck's novel *The Grapes of Wrath*. Filipino workers have told me that no workers were treated as poorly as the "Okies" and the "Arkies." Many of these people gained employment in the defense industry when World War II began.

Farmers demanded imported labor during the war, and the U.S. Government began to import *bracero* labor from Mexico. The *braceros* were Mexican nationals who held work permits for a specified period of time. The *bracero* program was intended as a stopgap measure during World War II and the Korean conflict, but political pressures kept the program alive until 1965, and extensions, for special cases, were made as late as 1967. The *braceros* were exploited beyond description by growers, labor contractors, and merchants. California churchmen and labor officials were responsible, in great part, for terminating the program. A book by Ernesto Galarza, *Merchants of Labor*, exposes many evils of the *bracero* program.

California has a history of intermittent and bitter farm-labor strikes. The Industrial Workers of the World (the "Wobblies") organized strikes at the turn of the century in California. The Wobblies met with repression from the police, vigilantes, and the government wherever they went.

Two strikers were killed by grower-vigilantes in the 1933 cotton strike in Pixely, just north of Delano. Over 18,000 workers were then on strike. The Cannery and

Agricultural Workers (CAWIU), a communist-backed union, continued its strike activities in the Imperial Valley in 1934.

I spoke to a veteran of the 1934 strike. He told me that the policy of the CAWIU was to avoid violence. "The same was not true of the sheriff's deputies and grower-vigilantes," he said. He reported that a young girl was suffocated to death by tear gas thrown into a farm workers' meeting hall. Strike leaders were gathered and put into a prison compound in the desert. The growers' official vigilante organization, the Associated Farmers, was subsequently founded, and it organized a citizens' army to attack lettuce strikers in Salinas, California, in 1936.

In 1939, the Associated Farmers put down another bitter strike against the Earl Fruit Company, a subsidiary of the Di Giorgio Corporation. Some of the strikers angrily referred to Sunkist Growers as "Gunkist," because they felt too much force had been used.

The National Farm Labor Union struck Di Giorgio's Arvin vineyards, near Bakersfield, California, in July, 1947. Over 1,000 workers walked out on strike, and the Associated Farmers took action once again. Di Giorgio recruited strikebreakers from Mexico. The corporation demonstrated its immense power by filing and winning lawsuits connected with a pro–farm worker film, *Poverty in the Valley of Plenty*.

A boycott of all Di Giorgio products was called, and the large chain of Safeway food stores no longer stocked Di Giorgio goods. In spite of the fact that farm workers were not covered under the National Labor Relations Act, a federal judge issued an injunction against secondary picketing. By the time the injunction was dropped, the strike had been effectively broken. One of the strike's leaders, Ernesto Galarza, has written a book about the struggle, *Spiders in the House and Workers in the Field*. Di Giorgio's immense wealth and the availability of strikebreakers and court injunctions were too much even for a union with nationwide support. It was not until 1966 that another union would exert the pressure that caused Di Giorgio to capitulate, turning the tide of farm-labor history in the United States. The setting was the Sierra Vista farms of the Di Giorgio Corporation, near the town of Delano.

Subsequent chapters will contain facts and figures on the immensity and power of California agribusiness, as well as the status of its labor force. The nerve center of the industry, according to writer Al Krebs, is located in the heart of San Francisco's financial district. It is there that the major decisions affecting food production and processing from the field to the table are made. But the corporate agricultural giants such as the Bank of America, the Pacific Gas and Electric Company, and the Wells Fargo Bank have now been joined by the conglomerates. The United Fruit Company, Purex, and Tenneco now have extensive farm holdings in California and in several other states.

Agribusiness is highly centralized in the southern San Joaquin Valley, where Delano is located. Eleven farming corporations alone control over 1 million acres of land. These growers receive huge subsidies for *not* growing certain crops. A prime example is J. G. Boswell, who controls over 100,000 acres of land in California alone. Boswell is on the board of directors of Safeway stores, which refused to cooperate in any way with the grape boycott. His Boston Ranch is located in Kings County near the town of Corcoran. It received $4 million in 1969 for *not* growing cotton.

In the winter of 1969, I supported the food protests held in Hanford, the Kings County seat. Many of the protestors were Boswell's workers. The Kings County Welfare Department refused to issue food stamps to hungry workers. Local ranchers and townspeople taunted the demonstrators at the courthouse, calling them lazy Mexicans and communist agitators. One of Boswell's cotton ranches receives $1,000 an acre in water subsidies from the federal government each year—on 37,555 acres of land!

The state's university system has been one of the major contributors to the wealth and growth of California agribusiness for decades. Anne and Hal Draper, of the University of California at Berkeley, have masterfully shown the industry's dependence on the university system in their well-written and thoroughly documented booklet "The Dirt on California." Millions of dollars in manpower and assistance have been channeled to the growers from the university, yet the farm workers have been completely ignored.

This was the scene then, dominated by conglomerates and landowners who are really big-time welfare babies, that Cesar Chavez and his followers confronted in the early 1960's. The members of his National Farm Workers Association had only a few dollars in their treasury. But they were eager to join their Filipino brothers, who had begun the longest and mostly costly farm-labor strike in U.S. history.

[3]

Viva la Huelga!

Viva la Huelga! is the battle cry of the Delano strikers. It has been heard on picket lines in the cold of the winter and in the summer's harvest sun, in front of supermarkets, in union halls, and at demonstrations and rallies throughout the nation. It will be heard across the land as long as farm workers lack the basic necessities to make life livable and enjoyable.

The Filipino workers began their strike in the vineyards near Delano on September 8, 1965. They were members of the Agricultural Workers Organizing Committee (AWOC), AFL-CIO. Their leader was Larry Itliong, a wiry, Mandarin-appearing Filipino with three fingers missing on one hand. The workers were receiving less than $1.20 an hour. They were demanding $1.40, plus 20 cents a box for their labor in the vineyards.

On September 16, Mexican Independence Day, Chavez's National Farm Workers Association (NFWA) voted to join the Filipinos. A joint strike committee was formed, and the Delano Grape Strike increased in intensity. Over 1,200 Mexican harvest hands left the vineyards in subsequent days. Charges of violence came from both sides, but most of the incidents were aggravated by hostile growers and foremen. Police, city officials, and Kern County sheriff's deputies made no secret of their antagonistic feelings toward the strikers. Delano became bitterly polarized. Merchants and small businessmen became vociferous in their denunciation of the strike.

Antiunion committees were formed, such as the Citizens for Facts and the Mothers Against Chavez, allegedly to show the subversive nature of the strike. Churchmen came from all parts of the United States to voice their support of the workers. The local clergy and growers retaliated with their own statements, defending self-interest and provincialism against the social gospel of the "outside agitators."

Local grape growers, headed by Martin Zaninovich and Bruno Dispoto, referred to the strike as a myth. Telegrams and registered letters asking for talks were returned unopened to strike headquarters. On December 1, grower-spokesman Joseph Brosmer turned down another NFWA plea for the state conciliation service to mediate the strike. Brosmer stated that farm workers negotiated with growers by their free choice to come to work each morning for their stipulated pay.

On December 17, Walter Reuther, at that time President of the United Auto Workers, arrived in Delano. Reuther pledged economic assistance to the strikers and full cooperation for any boycott action taken by the NFWA. The labor leader told strikers, "If General Motors had to change its mind because of the auto workers, then the growers will have to change their minds because of you, the farm workers. . . . Today it is no longer possible to exploit workers. You are leading history. We will march with you!"

Reuther spoke with prophetic insight when he predicted the future impact of the strike. "The human person is the core value of our society. Growers may believe this, but they are not applying this belief yet.

They will, because they will meet the full force of an aroused combination of unions, churches, and others concerned."

In February, 1966, when entertainer Steve Allen, a longtime friend of farm workers, supported the strike, Martin Zaninovich responded to the press: "The appearance of performer Steve Allen in Delano can only be interpreted as an effort to breathe some new life into a totally unsuccessful organizing attempt which is being promoted by a few self-appointed professional agitators. The mythical boycott has had no adverse effects on grapes and grape products from the Delano area."

In March, 1966, the U.S. Senate Subcommittee on Migrant Labor conducted an investigation of the Delano strike. The committee, represented by Senators Robert F. Kennedy, Harrison Williams, Democrat of New Jersey, and George Murphy, Republican of California, thoroughly questioned several witnesses. Bishop Hugh Donohoe, of Stockton, represented the Catholic bishops of California. Donohoe called upon the committee to include farm workers under the National Labor Relations Act. Coverage under the act enables the workers to elect a union to represent their interests. But, if there is no coverage, an employer can completely ignore the requests of his workers. This is essentially what the grape growers decided to do. The bishop also underscored the lack of health and safety legislation for farm workers and defended the right of farm workers to organize and strike. This infuriated the growers and their friends throughout the state.

An interesting exchange took place between Kennedy and the grower Martin Zaninovich during the hearings. Zaninovich claimed that farm workers in Delano did not want union representation. He added that farmers might accept elections if the proper machinery were present. Kennedy answered, "If we can go to the moon in the '60s, then we can surely set up machinery for elections, Mr. Zaninovich."

In March, 1966, the National Farm Workers Association began a historic march from Delano to Sacramento, the state capital. Meanwhile, as the demonstration progressed, the Schenley Vineyards Corporation of Delano agreed to recognize the NFWA. The Di Giorgio Corporation also agreed to hold elections.

On April 11, 10,000 farm workers and their supporters held a rally on the grounds of the State Capitol in Sacramento. Cesar and his followers were angry with Governor Edmund G. Brown for failing to appear at the gathering. Brown had made a previous commitment to be with his family in Palm Springs. The Reverend Chris Hartmire, Director of the California Migrant Ministry, told the crowd that Brown was in the wrong. "Many of us would have liked to be with our families on Easter," he said. "But here we are!"

Early in June, 1966, the Teamsters Union began an organizing drive among farm workers in the Delano area. But, due to pressure, especially from churchmen, the Teamsters agreed to stop their organizing campaign. The target of their efforts was the wealthy and extensive Di Giorgio Corporation. Late in June, the NFWA and AWOC withdrew their names from the ballot at the Di Giorgio ranch. Chavez told his members not to vote, because Di Giorgio employees were coercing many workers to vote for the Teamsters. In addition, strikers were not permitted to "trespass" on Di Giorgio property, and there had been many other irregularities connected with the election. Out of 732 workers, only 385 actually voted, and, of these, 291 voted for the Teamsters Union. Chavez's group challenged the election, and Cesar conferred personally with Governor Brown, seeking a new election. On July 14, Ronald Haughton, a labor relations expert appointed by Brown, called for a new election at Di Giorgio.

The Governor's cooperation with the farm-workers union angered the Teamsters. Their director of organization, William Grami, attacked Brown in the press and said the following about the NFWA: "The NFWA's organizing campaign is the greatest fraud ever perpetrated on the American public . . . the farm worker needs to be represented by a legitimate union, not to be used as a tool to build a power base for the New Left." Grami referred to his own union as "businesslike" and to the NFWA as "vicious and revolutionary in nature."

On August 1, 1966, Di Giorgio workers at the Sierra Vista and Borrego Springs ranches voted: 530 for NFWA, 331 for the Teamsters. The election proved that the majority of farm workers wanted a union and favored the Chavez group.

Chavez was later to endorse Governor Brown for re-election, especially "for his historic precedent-setting role in bringing about the first free and open elections for farm workers in the history of U.S. agriculture." Meanwhile, the Teamsters signed another back-door agreement, this time with the Perelli-Minetti vineyards, near Delano.

The NFWA merged with AWOC in August, 1966. The new organization was named the United Farm Workers Organizing Committee (UFWOC) and received a charter from the AFL-CIO. UFWOC declared a boycott against Perelli-Minetti and eventually won recognition from the firm in July, 1967. Through elections and car checks, UFWOC won recognition from several other wineries during this period: Christian Brothers, Jesuit Wines, Gallo, Paul Masson, Franzia, and others.

After lengthy discussions, mediated by a clergy committee from San Francisco, the Teamsters and UFWOC signed a mutual peace accord on July 22. The accord lasted until the Teamsters began to sign over 200 back-door contracts in the Salinas and Santa Maria valleys in the summer of 1970.

State Senator Hugh Burns, a conservative California Democrat, published a report on "Un-American Activities" in Delano in the fall of 1967. Even though the document admitted that communist influence in the strike was non-existent, Burns achieved his goal. Members of the John Birch Society still cling to the booklet as their bible. They are attracted to such phrases as, "Even though the Delano movement is not Communist-dominated, it lends itself to Communist-type influences."

Most grape growers declined to identify themselves with the extreme right wing. They openly vented their hostilities, however, at urban churchmen and members of the California Migrant Ministry, as well as students they portrayed as "long-haired, unwashed Berkeley-type agitators."

During the strike, the farm workers' newspaper, *El Malcriado* (literally, *The Bad Boy*), enraged many growers and citizens in Delano with its picaresque attacks against the injustices pervading the community. The paper, published in English and Spanish, combated grower propaganda and educated the workers on the significance of the strike. The structure of California agriculture and rural society was graphically portrayed by the skillful cartoons of Andy Zermeno. The growers were represented by *El Patroncito* (the boss), an obese, vulgar-looking man in sunglasses, wearing a panama hat. The labor contractors, many of whom are the worst enemies of the worker, were portrayed as *Don Coyote*. The workers were portrayed by *Don Sotaco,* a humble, downtrodden man, beaten by a cruel system. These three figures, pictured in different scenarios, helped educate the general public as to the moral, economic, and political issues of the strike.

I began my own involvement with the Delano strikers in the summer of 1967. Since that time, I have worked as a chaplain, boycott organizer, and now as the editor of *El Malcriado*. My work has met with stiff opposition from the clergy and initially from the hierarchy. It was only because of the intervention of the strikers and Cesar Chavez that I was allowed to remain in Delano. For their intercession, I will remain forever thankful.

When I arrived, the strike against Giumarra Vineyards, the largest table-grape growers in the world, had reached a stalemate. Picketing had been reduced by crippling injunctions, and the morale of the strikers was at a low ebb.

I never fully realized the tremendous sacrifices that the strikers had made until I began accompanying them on their picket lines. During the winter of 1967–68, the strikers would rise at 4:30 A.M. in order to picket the vineyards. Car caravans left Filipino Hall before dawn and headed to the farms where pruning operations were under way. By this time, the strikebreakers had become what the strikers called "hard-core scabs." They looked upon the strikers with contempt, thumbed their noses at the pickets, and made obscene gestures at the women strikers. At 8:00 A.M., the strikers returned home in order to send their children to school. They then reported to the union's offices to work until early evening.

I became discouraged and depressed at the lack of progress and the seeming hopelessness of the situation. I often wondered how the strikers could persevere against such great odds. Perhaps Manuel Chavez phrased it most accurately when he said, "We have nowhere to go but up." Manuel is Cesar's cousin and one of the union's top organizers.

Small events seemed to uplift the morale at times. We held Masses in the homes of the strikers. At Christmas time, caravans would come from all over the state, bringing food, clothing, and financial and moral support. The *Teatro Campesino* (Farm Workers' Theater) performed and depicted the struggle with perceptive and hilarious skits. The workers would sing "We Shall Overcome" and "Solidarity Forever" in Spanish.

In the early spring of 1968, Cesar feared that violence was an imminent danger. Pickets were harassed daily. The strikers had become jumpy and were beginning to feel defeated. On February 14, Cesar announced that he would begin a personal, religious fast. He left Filipino Hall alone and walked to Forty Acres, where he remained for twenty-five days without food. It was only at the insistence of his doctors that he then began to take nourishment.

Helen, Cesar's wife, told me why he fasted. "There had been some violence against the strikers," she said. "Some of the strikers had been shot at; their picket signs had been torn. Cesar felt there might be more violence."

Helen agreed with Cesar in principle, but she feared for his health. "People depended on Cesar. How could he do anything for the people, lying on a sickbed?" She told Cesar that the best thing he could do was to watch his health and encourage the people to keep fighting. "I was pretty upset," Helen continued. "But, when Cesar makes up his mind, nothing changes him."

The fast was effective in many ways. It brought the people together as a community. We offered Mass each night at the adobe gas station at Forty Acres. Although some strikers failed to see any significance in the sacrificial act, the majority of the workers supported Cesar. The forty-two-year-old leader said many times during the fast, "The workers understand. That's the important thing!"

There were soon over 500 people attending the services. Nationwide TV audiences caught the prayer, penance, and nonviolence themes of the fast. I am sure Cesar got his point across, and I am convinced that much of our present support was generated during that period.

The opposition called it a circus and labeled Cesar a fanatic and a showman. Clergymen I knew criticized Cesar for using a spiritual event as a tactic to win a strike. I argued with them that it was senseless to separate the moral and tactical elements associated with the fast. Sure it was a tactic! So were Gandhi's fasts and marches. They were courageous deeds, on behalf of nonviolence and directed at social change. Few men have the moral courage to perform such acts. Some find rhetoric and violence more acceptable, but, in the long run, that is a futile course.

On February 26, during his fast, Cesar had to appear in a Bakersfield court to face contempt-of-court charges imposed for alleged violation of an antipicketing injunction. Over a thousand farm workers and several clergymen surrounded the courthouse, singing the strike song *De Colores* and praying together. The judge and the entire staff at the courthouse were on edge. Jerry Cohen, the chief legal counsel for UFWOC, and I supported Cesar as we entered the building. He was extremely weak and barely made his way through the crowd. Newsmen and TV cameramen were tripping over each other as we made our way up an escalator to the courtroom. As we entered the courtroom, a very well-dressed and very hostile woman in her forties drew close to Cesar and spat out, "I hope you get what's coming to you, you son-of-a-bitch!" I later saw her leave the courthouse in a new Cadillac, which bore a bumper sticker that read, "America, Love It or Leave It!" The trial was postponed by the nervous and angry judge. The charges were later dropped.

The fast ended on March 11 with a Mass and a celebration at Delano's Memorial Park. Cesar, who had lost thirty-five pounds, sat weak and immobile next to Helen, his mother, and the late Senator Robert Kennedy. Several of my Franciscan confreres joined me in the celebration of the Mass. Others present were Fathers Jim Vizzard and Eugene Boyle, both long-time supporters of the movement. The Mass was ecumenical in nature. Jerome Lackner, Cesar's personal physician, read the first passage, from the Old Testament. Lackner is Jewish. A Protestant minister took the second reading, and a Catholic priest, the third. I later told a fellow priest that we are so ecumenical in Delano that Rome has not caught up with us yet.

Following the Mass, we distributed over three hundred loaves of Mexican *semita* bread. We blessed the bread and called it the bread of social justice. Several nuns in the congregation distributed it to the immense crowd. The Reverend Jim Drake, Cesar's administrative assistant and a member of the California Migrant Ministry, read a statement for Chavez. "Those who oppose us are rich and powerful," he began. "We are poor, but we have something the rich do not own—our bodies and our spirits and the justice of our cause. . . . Only by giving our lives do we find life. I am convinced that the truest act of manliness is to sacrifice ourselves for others in a totally nonviolent struggle for justice. To be a man is to suffer for others. God help us to be men."

Kennedy spoke amid the cheers of the workers. "I come here as an American citizen to honor Cesar Chavez," he said in a nasal Bostonian twang. "I honor him for his compassion, his honesty, his truth, and dedication." Kennedy's voice was drowned in applause as he called for equitable treatment of farm workers before the law. He said that farm workers had to be covered by the National Labor Relations Act, like other workers, and demanded tighter controls on aliens used as strikebreakers. He also praised the gains of UFWOC. "These are your victories," he said. "You won them with your hard work and with the leadership of people like Cesar Chavez!"

Paul Schrade, West Coast director for the United Auto Workers and a close friend of Cesar's, presented to the union a check for $50,000, on behalf of Walter Reuther. Reies Tijerina of New Mexico's *La Raza* movement was also in attendance. The fiery leader embraced Cesar during the Mass. Reporters tried unsuccessfully to extract an endorsement of violence from Tijerina, but he stated his support of Chavez and told newsmen that there were many ways to achieve justice.

I accompanied the Delano strikers during June, 1968, as they campaigned for Kennedy's primary in the East Los Angeles barrios. The Mexican-American vote in California was essential if Kennedy was to take California. After an exhausting three-day door-to-door precinct campaign, the farm workers made their way to the Ambassador Hotel for the victory rally.

Thousands of people packed the ballroom. Cesar became irritated and embarrassed when segments of the crowd began to shout, "We want Chavez!" His back was aching seriously. He retreated to a nearby church rectory to watch the proceedings on television.

Kennedy's tragic assassination occurred as the Senator was en route from the ballroom to an upstairs news conference. Since I was the only priest in attendance, I rushed to an exit when I heard rumors that Kennedy had been shot. People began to weep openly. I observed a woman throwing empty cocktail glasses against a wall in frustration, tears flowing down her cheeks. When I reached the outdoors, I spoke to one of Kennedy's campaign workers. He was sobbing with anger and frustration and kept repeating, "Bobby was the only man who could have united this country!" I asked him the whereabouts of the Senator. He pointed to an ambulance that was speeding away and told me that another priest had been inside the ambulance. Another ambulance arrived, and two more wounded men were loaded into the vehicle. Hours later, the farm workers were reunited at the Episcopal Church of East Los Angeles, our temporary headquarters.

I have never observed a sadder group of people in my entire life. The workers had a look of absolute despair on their faces. We gathered in prayer. A pall of silence hung over the strike for more than a week. This was abundant testimony of the devotion the workers had for Kennedy. A large segment of Delano's black population later joined us in a special memorial ceremony at Guadalupe church.

The summer brought with it a bitter strike in the Coachella Valley and an intensification of the international boycott of grapes.

The boycott struggle picked up momentum as more farm workers and volunteers were sent throughout the United States and Canada to spread the word of the strike. Their efforts are the subject of a later chapter. Suffice it to say that the initial cry of *Viva la Huelga!*, which rocked Delano in 1965 was heard by network TV five years later—Cesar Chavez and the Delano grape growers came to terms and signed one of the most significant collective bargaining contracts in U.S. labor history.

ESE CHUY, JESUS
(a young Chicano looks at Jesus and the church)

Ese Chuy, I don't go to *la iglesia, bato,*
because I have lost *la fe* in your church.
No, parale . . . Wait, *Chuy,* not in you, man.
I believe in you, *ese,* even if I don't know you,
porque la jefita always taught me that, *ese.*

Simon, Chuy; you are my real *jefito* . . .
and you are *a toda madre conmigo* when I need you.
But your *mendiga iglesia* is not for me, *carnal,*
your priests, *Chuy;* they talk about brotherhood, *ese,*
pero they don't know the meaning of it . . . *ni madre!*

Almost all of *la bola de padres* from your church, *ese,*
don't care about *batos locos* like me, not even *por la Raza.*
Solo que descontarlos or shape them up, *carnal* . . .
porque we are tired of those . . . *hipocritas!*
You know what you can do with them, so *hay te los dejo,*
     Chuy.

Bueno, that is all, *Chuy,* and *yo se que* you heard me.
You are right here listening to my *poema* about your
     padres.
I don't understand you and I cannot see you but you are
     here.
Solo que, change the *corazon* of those *padres, Chuy.*
te lo pide la jefita, la Raza and me, *ese* . . .
WHO STILL BELIEVE IN YOU.

(from *Poesias de la Causa,* by Juan A. Cuauhtemoc)

a toda madre conmigo: you are "right on" with me
bato: guy
batos locos: cool cats
la bola de padres: the bunch of Fathers
bueno: well
corazon: heart
ese, Chuy: Hey there, Jesus
la fe: faith
hay te los dejo: you can have them
la iglesia: the church
la jefita: mother
jefito: boss
mendiga iglesia: damn church
ni madre: nothing at all
parale: stop
pero: but
por la Raza: for the Chicanos
porque: because
simon, Chuy: like yeah, man
solo que: just
solo que descontarlos: just write them off
te lo pide: ask this of you
yo se que: I know that

[4]

The Churches
and the Struggle

"The churches *had* to get involved in this strike," Cesar said. "Everything they had taught for two thousand years was at stake in this struggle."

There are many reasons why the Catholic churches on the grass-roots level were slow to respond to the economic needs of farm workers, and especially to the strike. The chief goals of the church have been religious instruction and to provide the sacraments for the people. In the seminaries, little emphasis was given to the social teachings of the church as applied to the situation of farm workers in the Southwest. In addition to this, agricultural employers have exerted heavy financial and social pressures on the churches. There have also been many examples of authoritarian measures used by bishops to discipline priests involved in social reform. An excellent treatment of this subject is provided in a recent book, *The Mexican-American People,* by Leo Grebler, Joan W. Moore, and Ralph C. Guzman.

Two priests did pioneer work in California in the transition of the church toward more involvement with socio-economic problems. Their names are Fathers Thomas McCullough and Donald McDonnell. McDonnell was a close friend of Chavez's in the latter's early years as an organizer. Both priests received permission to work full-time with farm workers, but protests from growers and pastors eventually curtailed their work.

My own feelings about church involvement in the Delano strike remain somewhat ambivalent. At times, I have been profoundly discouraged at the callousness of my own church; on other occasions, I have been encouraged by its adaptability and concern for farm workers.

The California Migrant Ministry, under the direction of the Reverend Chris Hartmire, showed vigorous leadership in the farm workers' cause, even before the strike started. On October 19, 1965, the Reverend David Havens, of the Migrant Ministry, was arrested by Kern County sheriff's deputies for publicly reading Jack London's famous definition of a strikebreaker on a picket line. "A strikebreaker is a two-legged animal with a cork-screw soul, a water-logged brain and a combination backbone, made of jelly and glue," Havens read, as he was led away by the deputies.

On the next day, forty-four ministers and farm workers were arrested on another picket line near Delano's vineyards. The clergymen had come to Delano at Hartmire's request for a "Demonstration of Christian Concern."

The Migrant Ministry immediately became a target of attacks by growers and local ministers. Hartmire responded to the charges, saying that the church had to take a stronger stand for the poor when they attempted to help themselves. "We, in society, all benefit from poverty," he said. "We put light bandages over the wounds. Farm workers see us, in the church, as part of the establishment. We must do more than merely give food and milk to the hungry children of farm workers."

Just after the California Farm Bureau Federation had delivered a scathing attack on church involvement in the Delano dispute, eleven national church leaders arrived on the scene. Father James Vizzard, a feisty and articulate Jesuit, was the spokesman for the Catholic Church. He was accompanied by Monsignor William J. Quinn, of Chicago, another ardent supporter of the Chavez movement. The Protestant spokesmen were Stanford theologian Robert McAfee Brown and Kenneth Neigh, of the United Presbyterian Church of the United States. The Jewish faith was represented by Rabbi Erwin L. Herman of the Synagogue Council of America. They stated, "We reject the heresy that churches and synagogues are to be concerned only with 'spiritual matters.' The suffering of farm workers and their children cries to heaven and demands the attention of men of conscience."

Their statement supported the strike, since, according to their spokesman, "no other procedures have been opened to the workers." The clergymen called upon the growers to negotiate and asked for a congressional investigation of the Delano situation.

A few of the visitors had a heated meeting with Martin Zaninovich, who told them, "Our workers have rejected efforts of professional organizers to recruit them into unions. No union represents our workers." Zaninovich added that it was wrong for the men to fire up their congregations to send money to the strikers. Another grape grower, Jack Pandol, told the press, "The strike was a dead issue until church leaders stepped in to keep it alive."

The Delano Ministerial Association denounced the actions of the visiting clergymen and stated that it was not the function of churchmen to organize farm workers. They were supported in their contention by grape grower Bruno Dispoto, who said, "We are sincerely looking forward to the day when we get rid of outside agitators, rabble rousers, college kooks, migrant ministers and priests!"

On January 7, the Western Association of Reform Rabbis endorsed the grape strike and pledged aid to the strikers. They announced the initiation of a program to educate Reform Jews as to the plight of farm workers. Their spokesman, Rabbi Stephen Forstein, promised the active involvement of rabbis in the event of a grape boycott. Within a week, Rabbi Jack Levy, of Bakersfield, California, protested Forstein's statement, claiming that it did not represent the thinking of Jews in the area.

In January, the Most Reverend Aloysius J. Willinger, the Catholic Bishop of the Fresno diocese, denounced the Delano visit and statements of Father James Vizzard, of the National Catholic Rural Life Conference of Washington, D.C. He called the priest "The Hornblower of Delano" in the *Central California Register,* his diocesan newspaper. But Vizzard and two other priests, Fathers Eugene Boyle, of San Francisco, and Keith Kenny, of Sacramento, continued to support the strikers. Shortly after Willinger's action, the Episcopal Diocese of San Joaquin blasted the Migrant Ministry for behavior "inconsistent with the Church's role to preach the Gospel to all men."

In March, the California Council of Churches issued a statement defending the role of the Migrant Ministry in the strike. Ministry spokesman Dr. Paul Shelford said, "As Christians we cannot be neutral in the presence of social injustices which reduce the dignity and well-being of any of God's people. . . . We feel that the economic structures and the entire statewide community is responsible for the poverty of seasonal workers who live in an otherwise affluent society. The California Council of Churches commends the Reverend Chris Hartmire, the able director of the California Migrant Ministry. The Migrant Ministry has made a vital witness and has been a strong force for nonviolence during the struggle. . . . We believe as Christians that this situation has brought about a new opportunity to witness in this world."

Zaninovich was quick to respond to the statement: "I maintain that these clergymen [the Migrant Ministers] do not represent their congregations. I suggest that they hold secret ballots among their flocks to prove they do. Church leaders had better start looking for other financial means to carry out their radical ideas, which they are forcing upon us."

On April 22, the National Council of Churches, headed by Dr. Arthur Fleming, endorsed the strike. Several priests, rabbis, and ministers joined farm workers on their march to Sacramento.

When growers charged, to Hartmire, that the Migrant Ministry had done much harm to the good reputation of Delano, the minister responded, "The community of Delano is healthier now. It has undergone an operation. Other communities in the valley are the ones that are really sick. The wounds of resentment and unrest are hidden under a pall of silence. But the peace is false. Justice has yet to be accomplished."

One of the choicest comments regarding church activists in the Delano struggle was made by a diocesan church official in Sacramento, California. Father Eugene Lucas had been disciplined by his bishop, the Most Reverend Alden Bell, for picketing a market that sold struck grapes. Defending the bishop's action, the official stated, "The Church feels that such picketing is the role of the layman and not that of the Church." I believe that the statement is a collector's item and should be carefully analyzed by anyone concerned with the role of the church in society.

Support from all the major religious communities increased as the strike and the boycott became better publicized throughout the country. Financial and moral support came from all segments of the major faiths as the boycotters visited churches and synagogues, telling their story.

Catholic church groups made a no-interest loan to UFWOC to defray the expenses of the Salinas strike in 1970. The Franciscans donated an elaborate printing oper-

ation called Serra Press to the movement. I have been
gratified by the continued generosity and support of the
friars for *la causa.*

During the strike, Cesar frequently made references to
the social teachings of the Catholic Church. He was forced
to conclude, however, that these documents had been confined to theory and seldom put into practice. "The church
has lost the working classes in Europe, and it may very well
lose large segments of the working class in this country too,
unless something drastic is done."

I asked Cesar about his feelings toward the church one
evening when he and his wife, Helen, had supper at Guadalupe church rectory with me and some visiting priests.
"Most farm workers are Chicanos," Cesar said. "And most
Chicanos are Catholics. The church is the only institution
which our people are closely associated with. When the
church does not respond to us, we get very offended, and
we are tempted to lash out against it.

"You know," he continued, "there are many changes in
the church today. But many of these changes, like the new
ritual of the Mass, are merely external. What I like to see
is a priest get up and speak about things like racism and
poverty. But, even when you hear about these things from
the pulpit, you get the feeling that they aren't doing anything significant to alleviate these evils. They are just talking about them.

"Here in Delano, the church has been such a stranger to
us, that our own people tend to put it together with all
the powers and institutions that oppose them."

Cesar paused for a moment, then said, "But I think
that a storm is brewing with the Mexican American and
the church. Unless something is done very soon, the church
leadership is going to have a hell of a time.

"I've been at this work for twenty years, and I've taken
a lot of guff from priests. There have been a few good
priests. But most of them have opposed me. I don't get too
angry about it, though. I know that there are all kinds of

people in the church. I love the church. Instead of getting angry, I feel very depressed and pained.

"You know," he continued, his eyes opening wider, "the church could really help the Chicanos right now. It could change the social order for the better. It could really be in the forefront of a revolution for human dignity. I don't want to see the people walk away from it. But it's happening, you know."

It has been a bewildering experience to see priests openly side with growers against unionism in agriculture, completely ignoring the social doctrine of the church. The doctrine, based on the inherent dignity of the individual created by God, became prominent during the rapid industrialization of Europe. At that time, industrialists denounced Pope Leo XIII for defending the rights of workers to establish organizations for better wages and working conditions. Forty years later, Pius XI wrote that workers had a God-given right to organize and to strike when necessary. Recent popes have developed this doctrine to embrace all the struggling minority groups throughout the world. John XXIII had a soft spot in his big heart for the working man and boasted of being the son of a farm worker. Paul VI, considered by many to be a conservative, took radical stands on the sharing of wealth in his encyclical letter *The Progress of Peoples.* Quoting Saint Ambrose, Pope Paul said, "The world is given to all, not only to the rich."

The documents of the Second Vatican Council laid a heavy emphasis on justice rather than paternalism. They condemned any false separation of things spiritual from the material concern of men for their daily bread. They strongly denounced any notion of religion as a "pie in the sky" pursuit. The focal point of the *Pastoral Constitution of the Church in the Modern World* was "man himself, whole and entire, body and soul, heart and conscience, mind and will."

The Catholic bishops of the United States referred to the

social teachings of Vatican II, when they made their statement on farm labor in 1968. Subsequently, they formed the Bishops Farm Labor Committee. The outstanding contribution of this committee is the subject for a later chapter in this book.

My concern, nevertheless, has been to change the church on the local level so that it will meet the needs of the poor in a constructive way. Perhaps ways can be devised to rid the church of the sacred cow of clericalism. Perhaps strong leadership can be developed among the people who have most need of the power and resources of the church.

I'm not sure how these things can be accomplished. In the meantime, the church's most powerful presence will be manifested on picket lines and wherever the struggle for justice is waged. The best offering the church can make is a spirituality that places an emphasis on meeting human needs and does not simply further its own institutions. If this spirituality exists in a vacuum, alongside injustices and misery, and if it does not have a dynamic relationship with the alleviation of social evils such as poverty, war, and racism, then it is simply worthless.

[5]

Delano:
A Steak Dinner or
a Plate of Beans?

Helen Chavez looks weary as she finishes her office work. It is late afternoon in the winter of 1969. The wife of Cesar Chavez is working in a house converted into the offices of the Farm Workers Credit Union and Service Center. Some field workers patiently wait in the crowded offices for the small loans that will carry their families a little further along—perhaps until the rain stops.

Helen leaves the office at 5:30 P.M. in order to cook supper for Cesar and her seven children. Cesar is confined to bed with a serious back condition. Five people are packed into his bedroom-office. Cesar is sitting up. He is engaged in a phone call to Eliseo Medina in Chicago, one of the union's most promising young organizers. Eliseo reports that the largest chain stores in the Chicago area have agreed not to handle grapes. There is only one boxcar shipment of grapes in the Windy City, a phenomenal drop from the previous year.

Cesar encourages Eliseo, telling him to continue to seek the help of organized labor, housewives, church leaders, and other activists. He tells him that the Delano growers had to dump a lot of rotten grapes from their cold storage at a heavy financial loss. If the early grapes from California's Coachella Valley and from Arizona do not find markets this June, the growers will be forced to sign. Some of them are already asking for exploratory meetings. Things are looking better.

Volunteers Marion Moses and Leroy Chatfield begin to discuss the new health-and-welfare plan they have just spent months in preparing. The new program, called the Robert F. Kennedy Memorial Plan, embraces the ranches covered by collective-bargaining agreements. For the first time in the history of American agriculture, employers will contribute—ten cents an hour for each worker—into a health-and-welfare fund. The plan offers everyday family care, doctors' visits, and X-ray, blood, urine, and cancer tests. It also offers medicine, maternity benefits, and small hospital cash benefits. Marion and Leroy agree that, in addition to its immediate benefits, the plan will be priceless as an organizing tool. With Cesar's help, they outline a week-long schedule of visits to the farms in order to explain the plan to each ranch committee.

An hour later, Cesar's eyes begin to look heavy with fatigue. The meetings had begun early in the morning, just after I brought the Eucharist to the Chavez family. Cesar's brother Richard and Rudy Ahumada leave him about 10:00 P.M. They had been outlining plans for a new accounting system for the Service Center.

At 10:30, the attorneys for the United Farm Workers Organizing Committee, Dave Averbuck and Jerry Cohen, meet with Cesar to discuss the day-long pesticide hearings in the Bakersfield Superior Court. The two young lawyers

had been attempting to get access to public records on the use of pesticides by farmers. Pesticide-company officials had obtained a restraining order to protect their business interests and "trade secrets." The company sells the deadly poisons now being used on Kern County crops. Countless workers have been coming into the union's clinic with skin diseases, nerve disorders, and respiratory ailments caused by parathion and tetraethylpyrophosphate (TEPP). Few studies have been done to measure the harmful effects of these deadly poisons. Jerry remarks that an executive from the pesticide company admitted that he would never use parathion on his own farm. Why not? It is too dangerous. He will sell it to other growers, however, and at an astounding profit! But no one must gain access to any trade secrets. After all, would the Coca-Cola Company give away its formula? Jerry Cohen reminded the judge that one-seventieth of a teaspoon of Coca-Cola will do little harm. But the same amount of parathion will kill a man, even on skin contact.

Dave Averbuck points out to Cesar, during a recess in court, that he had overheard the agricultural commissioner of Kern County speaking to a pesticide-company representative. "Don't use the public restroom," the official had said. "Use the one marked 'Employees.' The public restroom is full of those damn Mexicans." He was referring to the farm workers who had come to testify regarding pesticide poisoning.

Cesar listens attentively to the attorneys. He has just written a public letter to the grape industry on the pesticide issue, which concluded, "We will not tolerate the systematic poisoning of our people."

Cohen shows Cesar the affidavits taken from several workers in Kern and Tulare counties. Mr. and Mrs. Abelardo de Leon, of Porterville, were working with their son Juan and daughter Maria on a farm owned by the Bank of America. They stated that spray rigs were using a deadly poison while the crew was working. Mr. de Leon said that he began to itch all over his body. Rashes appeared, his eyes became irritated, and he began to suffer stomach pains and vomit. He was forced to receive medical treatment, which his bosses refused to pay for. Mrs. de Leon had to stop working because her eyes were red and swollen. When the family complained about this to their foreman, Manuel Armendarez, he laughed and called them "crybabies."

Francisca and Ruben Barrientos, of Plainview, complained about eye irritation and skin rashes due to the pesticides sprayed while they were working with oranges. The foreman told them that, if they didn't like it, they could quit. Mr. Barrientos then began to work in the vineyards. The poisonous residues on the vines caused the skin on his hands to become covered with rashes, while his fingernails blackened and began to chip and fall off.

And when Dolores Vierra and her friends were working on the Richardson ranch near Lamont, they were sprayed with a deadly poison, causing the usual symptoms. She asked the owner why they were spraying so close to the workers. He replied with a laugh, "The spray makes grapes grow bigger, and it will make the women's breasts bigger, too!"

When Elivorio Cisneros worked on a ranch near Parlier, California, a grower told him to spray the vines with a parathion solution. The instructions on the label stated that one quart was to be diluted with 600 gallons of water. But the grower told Cisneros to dilute a quart with 100 gallons of water, producing a poison six times stronger than that directed. Cisneros drove the tractor all day. When he arrived home that night, he could not sleep. He was seriously ill the next day. His vision was impaired, and his stomach was upset. He was nearly unconscious when he arrived at the doctor's office. Two farm workers were to die in the summer of 1970 from similar parathion poisoning in the tobacco fields of the Deep South.

Hundreds of affidavits had been taken. Invariably, serious skin disorders were in evidence, as well as dizziness and visual disturbances. The workers had been sprayed while working, in open defiance of pesticide regulations. Almost always, the grower would minimize the condition of the workers and refuse them medical attention.

It is getting late. It is past midnight. Cesar speaks about present problems in the union, its future goals. He reaffirms the need for a firm ethical and nonviolent base. He whispers so as not to awaken the children. The last visitor leaves at 1:30 A.M. The lights go out. The flame from the gas heater dances reflections on the wall. A cold wind sprinkles rain against the windows.

The next day brings more meetings—long, intense sessions about bookkeeping and the union's finances. In the early afternoon, three rabbis from the San Francisco Bay area come to meet with Cesar and later with some of the Delano growers. They are unimpressed with the weak rationalizations of the growers who refuse to negotiate with their employes. At 3:00 P.M., Cesar's teen-age daughters return from school and have something to report to their father. Anna, Eloise, and Linda had gone to Kingsburg on a school trip to visit a raisin-processing plant. When they arrived at the entrance to the plant, they noticed that a picket line had been set up to protest the poor wages and working conditions of the shed workers. The girls demanded that the bus driver let them off at the gate. They spent over an hour picketing until the bus returned for them. Their father smiles approvingly. He is proud of them.

Later on in the afternoon, a magazine writer interviews Cesar. He quizzes him about a training program in nonviolence he is planning for his organizers. Cesar insists that the program cannot be academic or classroom-oriented. It has to be a kind of on-the-job training, and an embodiment of the spirit of nonviolence. The trainee learns from example and by assimilation. Nonviolence is not merely a clever technique to be used on special occasions. The thoroughly nonviolent person sees purposeful acts of sacrifice, cleaning floors and toilets or preparing meals and fasting, as part of his training and part of his life. When he sees before him the option of eating a steak dinner or sharing a plate of beans with a poor family, he chooses the latter.

Cesar explains how he and his brother Manuel learned how generous the poor could be. Several years ago, they had no money but felt ashamed to beg for gas and food. They found themselves in the small cotton-gin town of Corcoran. Cesar mustered as much courage as he could and looked for the poorest house in the neighborhood.

Children were running about everywhere, playing with cats and dogs. The two men humbly asked for a bite to eat. They explained that they were organizing farm workers to help the people get better pay and a better life for their families. The woman of the house greeted them with a friendly smile and said that the men were out chopping cotton. She told them that supper was almost ready—and would they stay? After supper, the men chatted late into the night. They described the many agricultural strikes of their lifetimes to the young organizers. They vividly re-called the cotton strike of 1933, when the farmer-vigilantes raided the union hall in Pixely and fired on the workers, killing two of them. Cesar and his brother had made valu-able friends at that time. One of them, Julio Hernandez, is now an officer in the union.

Later on in the afternoon, a call comes from Los Angeles. Some of the union's officers have met with representatives of the Coachella Valley grape growers. The union demands immediate recognition this time, not elections. It had al-ready offered elections during the last harvest season, but the growers had refused. We discover that the grape grow-ers in the Coachella Valley (near Palm Springs) are very worried that they will not have a market for their early grapes in June because of the boycott. The meetings prove to be a ray of hope. At the present time, the workers are starving for signs of hope and progress. The 1967 and 1968 harvest seasons had come and gone with no breakthroughs.

Cesar speaks of laying the groundwork for a strike in June in Coachella. His close associates agree with him that it is up to the growers to make the next move.

Memories of last summer's strike in Coachella are recounted—the long hot days under the desert sun; the frustrating feeling everyone had, when, just as things looked promising, busloads of strikebreakers came across the border from Mexicali. History repeated itself. Once again, poor people were brought in to be used in exploiting and oppressing other poor people. And all of this in order to enrich a few affluent agribusinessmen who sat in comfortable offices in San Francisco. Memories rush to mind— memories of the strikers rising at 3:00 A.M., of picket captains leading caravans of broken-down jalopies to the vineyards, their headlights piercing the predawn darkness near Thermal and Coachella; memories of John Birch Society members passing out hate literature at the Greyhound bus station and in front of the Catholic church—in front of the Catholic church where the local pastor did not want to get "involved" but later openly manifested his antiunion feelings. Memories of a strike that was partially successful— memories of promises that the union would be there again in the 1969 harvest season to finish the job; memories of the grateful smiles and warm embraces of the local farm workers and of the hostile stares of local residents, bankers, politicians, and growers; memories of Cesar telling the workers at an evening rally, "No, I am not a communist. But I'm not saying this because people are accusing me of being one. I'm saying this because I'm a Christian, and I'm proud of that!"

In spite of the slow pace of the struggle, a great deal of progress has been made since the strike vote in 1965. Martin Luther King spoke of a dream he had, a vision of the future. There was another fellow who had a dream too. His name was Tom Joad, the legendary protagonist of John Steinbeck's novel *The Grapes of Wrath*. Tom had migrated with his family from Oklahoma to California in the 1930's. Toward the end of the story, Tom gets involved with farm-labor organizers and is hunted down like a criminal. He tells his mother about his dream of the future. He says, "Ma, I'll be there, whenever there's a fight so that hungry people can eat—I'll be there. I'll be there wherever there's a cop beating up a guy. I'll be there in the way guys yell when they're mad, and I'll be there in the way kids laugh when they're hungry and they know supper's ready.

"And when our folks eat the stuff they raise and live in the houses they build—why I'll be there. See? Ma, See?"

Tom had disappeared into a maze of vines, and his mother never saw him again. But his dream is finally coming true. Farm workers are finally being treated with dignity. They have finally succeeded in building a power base whereby they can determine the course of their own lives.

After several hundred attempts to organize farm workers in California; despite overwhelming odds, vigilantism, the staggering might of banks, farming corporations, and land companies; despite hostile state and local governments, discrimination in the courts and law-enforcement agencies; and despite repeated red-baiting and smear campaigns, the tiny union has survived and grown.

Despite a total lack of bargaining machinery and protection under federal and state law; despite a superabundance of strikebreakers, which our government helps recruit annually, the union has won every election it has ever held.

Unionized farm workers are now providing for their families in ways they had never before thought possible. They are building their own homes and will soon reap the benefits of the new health-and-welfare program.

It is already evening. Helen has returned home from the credit union office with her daughters. Anna and Eloise help her each day after school. Supper has been served, and the younger Chavez children play with a puppy in the living room.

More reports come in from volunteers who have arrived in new boycott cities—Miami, Houston, Kansas City, Memphis, and Phoenix. Labor and church groups have been generous with their support. A meeting begins to discuss the campaign against Safeway, the most powerful food chain in the West. Petitions are being circulated to student, labor, church, and community groups. They call upon Safeway not to handle California grapes. The campaign is headed by Fred Ross, a veteran organizer and close friend of Cesar and his family.

The lights go out in the Chavez house about midnight. Cesar has just put down a magazine. It is opened to a middle section. There is a picture of a dear friend, the late Senator Robert F. Kennedy. Below his picture is a quote from a speech he delivered to a group of eager college students:

> Each time a man stands up for an ideal, or acts to improve the lot of others, or strikes out against injustice, he sends forth a tiny ripple of hope, and crossing each other from a million different centers of energy and daring, these ripples build a current that can sweep down the mightiest walls of oppression and resistance.

[6]

Farm Workers: Their Long Road to Victory

Marching, Striking, and Boycotting

In 1969, I helped farm workers distribute leaflets in front of the farmers' market in Los Angeles. People's reactions are heightened when they see a priest or a nun picketing in religious garb. Most people accepted the leaflets with a smile; others ignored us with what appeared to be hostility mixed with fear. The leaflet featured a picture of a typical worker's shack in the San Joaquin Valley. Seated on a bed in the dwelling was a small Mexican-American girl, her clothes in tatters. A bare light bulb hung from the ceiling of the weather-beaten dwelling. Below the photo was a caption: "Please help farmworkers. Do not buy California grapes." An elderly gentleman received a leaflet, then tore it to shreds and threw it on the pavement. "Why don't her ol' man become a plumber?" he spat out.

I recall another occasion, when we picketed a Loblaw's supermarket in Toronto. Several prominent labor and church leaders joined us on the picket line. Included on the line were some very dedicated Teamsters—the kind of union men that fit the description "the salt of the earth." On this occasion, the young check-out clerks became very hostile and began eating grapes next to our picket line. The Teamsters became furious. One of them, a giant of a man nicknamed "The Bear," tried to control his brothers who were ready for a brawl. I was asked to intervene. While I asked the grape-eaters to finish their meal inside the store, one of the union men was in the process of inviting a clerk "around back." I canceled this meeting, tried to calm the fellow down, and kept the picket line moving. "I'll murder that guy, Father," he said. "How can those goddamn scabs eat grapes while those kids out in California nearly starve to death?" As he was speaking, the executive secretary of the Ontario Labor Federation had invited the young clerks for some coffee at a nearby lunchstand. He and I spoke to the boys, explaining the background of the strike and boycott. The boys were themselves union members but completely uneducated about the labor movement. I admired the skill and gentleness of the union official as he explained the grape strike and boycott. In the end, they were won over to the cause.

In the cities I worked on as a boycott organizer, we used every possible technique to win the support of the public. We had a sit-in at the headquarters of the Jewel Tea Company near Chicago. Housewives wrote postcards and placed phone calls to the A & P executive offices in Philadelphia. In Toronto, we had a balloon-in at several supermarkets. Helium-filled balloons with "Boycott Grapes" painted on them would be released in the stores. On another occasion, we handed out similar balloons to children in the stores.

Have you ever seen a clerk try to relieve a child of a
balloon?

The grape boycott gained widespread support as the 1969
grape harvest season arrived in Coachella. During the
strike, we rose each morning at 3:30 to eat a quick breakfast and join the picket line. By 9:00 A.M., the temperature
was well above 100 degrees. The growers were arrogant.
It was clear that they had no intention of signing contracts
until they became financially imperiled. We could see that
most of the workers felt guilty about crossing our picket
lines. Those who walked out won the respect of the rest of
the strikers.

Farm workers are frequently romanticized. The worker
is pitted against the grower and vice-versa in a good guy–
bad guy situation. But even when one observes the ambi-
guities and the pros and cons of both sides, it is easy to draw
a few simple conclusions. No matter how many exceptions
one may find, the worker is exploited and abused when he
works without the protection of a union. He receives a
miserable wage, and he has absolutely no job security. The
strikers knew this. The strikebreakers knew this too. The
growers knew it only too well. They realized that the system they were perpetuating was bad and that change would
be inevitable. Mike Bozick was one of the employers who
decided to fight hard and tough. But, in the end, the boycott caught up with him, and he had to admit it. Bozick
finally signed a contract in July, 1970.

During the summer of 1970, the Coachella grapes went
to the market and growers suffered a tremendous loss because of boycott pressures. The Arvin, Lamont, and Delano crops likewise suffered from low prices and no
demand at the market place. A prominent Kern County
grape grower stated in midsummer, 1970, "You people
now have the industry on a downhill pull. The rest of the
grape growers will sign without a doubt. The boycott has
worked fantastically well."

Cesar Chavez told a national television news team that

UFWOC faced the task of consolidating its gains after signing the bulk of the grape industry in summer, 1970. The rest of America's poor looked on as farm workers won their most significant gains in history. A boycott had worked, and it offered hope to millions.

The Long Road

For decades, our nation's farm workers were a silent minority. In the 1930's, health studies, Senate investigating committees, and novelists began to shed light on the plight of this forgotten segment of our society. Libraries were filled with charts and graphs, statistics, migration routes, and case studies. But the conscience of America was not really awakened until farm workers took up picket signs and banners and marched in six different states demanding justice for themselves and their families.

Their most notable march was to Sacramento, California in spring, 1966. Their most recent pilgrimages took them nine days—from Coachella, California to the international border at Calexico in May, 1969.

The purpose of the march to Calexico, according to Pete Velasco, Filipino director of organization for the 1969 campaign in Coachella, was to appeal to our brothers in Mexico to join us in our struggle. "We are asking them not to break our strike," Velasco said, "so that all of us will get better wages and a union contract with the growers. As it is now, the growers pit brother against brother in order to break our union." Velasco was referring to Mexican workers who commute to work in the United States on a temporary visa. They are used by grape growers as strikebreakers. Until now, little has been done by lawmakers or government agencies to halt this practice.

The march began on Saturday, May 10, with an outdoor Mass at the Indio labor camp near Coachella. The marchers were farm workers who would later strike the vineyards around Coachella, Thermal, and Mecca, California. They listened to a proclamation read to them by one of the organizers. It read: "We who till the soil and harvest the crops of the border regions to the south of this nation will no longer be divided from our brothers living in Mexico. For too long, ranchers have devised methods to set us against one another. For too long, we have been used by selfish exploiters who have bent our backs to produce their riches. But now we say, ENOUGH! Enough of our mutual enslavement to wealthy employers who live like kings for a year on the product of our season's sweat.

"We proclaim our solidarity with our brothers to the south. We appeal to them to march with us . . . fight with us for the bread of social justice. We proclaim that henceforth we shall do nothing apart that can be done as well together.

"In the words of the Plan of Delano, we say, 'We do not want the paternalism of the rancher; we do not want the exploitation of the labor contractor; we do not want charity at the price of dignity. We want to be equal with all the working men in the nation; we want a just wage, better working conditions, and a decent future for our children.'

"To those who oppose us, be they ranchers, police, politicians, or speculators, we say that we are going to continue to fight—together—until we die, or we win. *Nosotros Venceremos.* We shall overcome."

The temperature soared into the hundreds as the band of some seventy workers and their families headed south on Highway 111. Each marcher was given a copy of the rules: "Obey the orders of the captain. Drink water sparingly. Do not wander from the line without permission. Do not talk back to agitators. Keep cool, baby, keep cool. Be cheerful. We are on the road to victory."

The wisdom of the rules soon became apparent. Large, heavily laden semitrucks would pass by at high speeds only a few feet from the marchers. Most of the truckers gave the pilgrims the victory signal and a blast on their air horns.

As the march traveled southward, there were no more

palm groves, vineyards, or citrus orchards. There would be desert now, bounded on the west by the Salton Sea, for the next fifty miles. The marchers would camp twice on the shores of the Salton Sea.

Two vehicles followed the marchers. One was a makeshift ambulance driven by a volunteer nurse. The other was the water truck, tended by Nicasio Campos, a striker from Coachella.

The marchers had been reminded that this would be a pilgrimage of penance. The heat and blisters soon made this clear to them. Cesar Chavez had frequently told them that a union is built on suffering and sacrifice. There are no short cuts. "Nothing worthwhile is ever won without suffering. To be a man is to suffer for others. God help us to be men," he told his followers during his twenty-five-day fast. Chavez also knew that the march would discipline the Coachella strikers and help them understand the meaning of nonviolence. The march was to form them into a community of purpose and concern. Later on, during the strike, the strength and depth of this community became obvious.

José Uribe, sixty-five years of age and father of seven strikers, told me what *la causa* had done for his people. "Before, the workers always held their heads down. They were afraid of everyone. Now they hold their heads high. Señor Chavez has taught our people not to be afraid. He taught us that there is hope, and he showed us how to reach out for it."

There was an exodus motif to the march, heightened by the fact that the grape pickers were marching through desert terrain probably very similar to the territory in the Near East. A people that had lived for decades in bondage and exploitation were on a Passover march. They were heading for a kind of Promised Land, where the burdens of farm work would be a bit lighter, thanks to collective bargaining. No contract, however, could take the slavery out of picking wine grapes or the heat out of the cruel San Joaquin Valley sun. But farm workers had already con-

quered their worst enemy, fear. They would never return
to its darkened shores. Their pride and determination
would lead them to victory.

As the workers reached the small towns in the Imperial
Valley, they were warmly greeted by the local workers. The
Catholic priests in Niland and Brawley were generous in
their support of the pilgrims, lending parish facilities for
cooking and lodging. The priest in Niland went so far as
to offer his own bed to three children, exhausted from the
long trek.

On the morning of the eighth day of the march, the
Reverend Ralph Abernathy of the Southern Christian
Leadership Conference joined the pilgrimage. He praised
the courage and leadership of Cesar Chavez, referring to
him as "that noble saint." He marched the entire morning
and pledged that SCLC would help the farm workers.

During the last two days of the march, the number of
participants grew from seventy-five to close to five hundred.
Farm workers, students, housewives, ministers, priests, and
nuns carried banners, sang, and shouted: *Viva la Huelga!
Viva la Causa! Viva Cesar Chavez!*

Just outside Calexico, a busload of television and movie
entertainers arrived from Hollywood. Another group
joined them minutes later: Senators Walter Mondale,
Democrat of Minnesota, and Ralph Yarborough, Democrat of Michigan.

Mondale, the chairman of the Senate Subcommittee on
Migratory Labor, shook hands across the international border with a Mexican official. The official stated, "There are
different positions on the strike here in Mexico." Mondale
replied, "Well, I'm on the side of Cesar Chavez and the
United Farm Workers Organizing Committee!"

The march ended with a rally in a Calexico park. Cesar
Chavez and Senator Edward Kennedy, of Massachusetts,
addressed the crowd. Kennedy said that he came because
he heard the voice of his brother Cesar Chavez. He stated
that any country that could send men to the moon could
certainly improve the lot of farm workers. The crowd was

vibrant with enthusiasm. The strikers returned home with the conviction that 1969 was to be the year of the farm worker.

A new ray of hope came with the morning paper three weeks later. According to the large headlines in the June 14 edition of the *Los Angeles Times,* "GROWERS SEEK TO END GRAPE STRIKE." The feature story, by labor editor Harry Bernsteins, reported that a small group of table-grape growers had agreed to negotiate with the union. This group was later criticized by the rest of the industry.

Martin Zaninovich, a Delano grower and president of the reactionary South Central Farmers Committee, denounced the negotiations. In a prepared statement, he and other grower spokesmen underscored the participation of "leftists" in the grape boycott and concluded, "We will not sell out the American consumer or our workers to Chavez or anyone else's coercive tactics. . . ."

The same opinion was reflected in an NBC-TV interview with Mike Bozick, head of the Desert Grape Growers and a prominent Coachella grower. He had previously referred to the march as another "futile Chavez publicity stunt." He added that there were no real farm workers on the march and that the entire pilgrimage was a sham.

Immediately following his statement, the NBC cameras showed ten-year-old Pedro Esquivel limping along Highway 111 on blistered feet. Behind him walked his father and sisters. Their faces shone with hope and determination. They were fighting the wealth and power of the affluent grape industry with their bodies and the justice of their cause. During the past year, hundreds of families like them had presented their case to the American housewife. The final victory was being won in the supermarkets throughout the country. The American public was informing California growers that it chose not to buy the grapes of wrath.

Meanwhile, the Esquivels and thousands of other farm workers were continuing their long march to victory, remembering the words of their leader, Cesar Chavez: "Time accomplishes for the poor what money does for the rich."

[7]

The Black Eagle
and the Grapes
of the Desert

It is 5:00 A.M. in the small town of Coachella, California.
The sun is beginning to rise, outlining the rugged desert
hills against the sky. The only signs of life are carloads of
farm workers arriving at the offices of the United Farm
Workers Organizing Committee.

The headquarters, formerly a Pentecostal church, was
rented a few months earlier. Along the eaves of the run-
down edifice is written: *Campesinos, unidos venceremos,
dividos caeremos! Viva la Causa! Viva Coachella!*—CESAR
CHAVEZ. (Fellow workers, united we shall overcome, divided we fall. Long Live the Cause! Long Live Coachella!)
Under the black eagle is written in large letters: United
Farm Workers, Coachella Union Local.

A breakfast of rolls and coffee is being served to the
strikers. They are farm workers and their families from the

valley, dissatisfied with their pay and working conditions, eager to man the picket lines. Only a week ago, they completed a 100-mile march to the Mexican border to solicit support for their cause. It is now May 27, 1969, the second day of the strike. Pete Velasco, the director of organization for the Coachella campaign, has assembled the families for a briefing before they set out for the vineyards. Two picket captains, Nicasio Campos and Alfredo Vasquez, are securing a loudspeaker to the roof of a car. This is the most valuable means of communication available between the picket line and the workers, who are often hidden inside the vineyards by the growers and crew bosses.

A radio in one of the strikers' jalopies is blaring out a song, *Adelita*, a ballad of the Mexican Revolution. The style of the music is *norteña*, the polka-like rhythm of northern Mexico. An announcer of the Mexicali radio station interrupts the song for a message to all farm workers: "Cesar Chavez asks all his brothers from across the border, 'Please do not break the grape strike in the Coachella Valley. The strike will benefit all workers on both sides of the border. We ask you to respect the picket lines of the United Farm Workers.' " The music begins again, this time with the violins and trumpets of a *mariachi* and a song of unrequited love from the south of Mexico.

Reports come in telling of the exact location of the crews working in the vineyards. Within minutes the thirty-car caravan of strikers, consisting of cars and pickups, heads for the grape-picking area.

José Uribe and fifteen-year-old Freddie Gamez accompany me in my car. José points to a nearby police car and tells me in Spanish, "They are beginning to accept us now. They always gave us a lot of trouble in the past."

A rancher's pickup truck speeds past us and crosses the railroad tracks that separate us from the vineyards. On his two-way radio, he will undoubtedly warn those ahead that the strikers are on their way.

As we cross the tracks, we have a good view of the citrus

orchards, vineyards, and palm groves in the early glow of
dawn. A slight breeze lifts the palm fronds, gently. There
is scattered evidence that man has intruded and conquered
the desert to grow these crops. Here and there we see sand
and rocks and cactus and are reminded that only sixty years
ago nothing could grow here. The leaflets from the Chamber of Commerce tell how it all happened. Water was
brought in from the Colorado River and technological
know-how from the University of California. But nothing
is said about the migratory laborers: the Filipinos, the
Mexicans, the dust-bowlers, and others. Nobody wants to
shoulder the guilt for building an agricultural empire on
human misery and exploitation.

The majority of the workers now are Mexicans and
Mexican Americans. As the sun begins to send its rays
over the valley of Coachella, hundreds of these harvest
hands set out to pick its $13.5 million grape crop. During
the next six weeks, they will encounter picket lines set up
by their fellow workers. They will hear the cries *"Viva la
Huelga!"* and *"Viva Cesar Chavez!"* The drama of the
Coachella grape strike of 1969 will unfold. And it will
extend to all parts of the United States, Canada, and Europe—to wherever grapes are sold, and boycotted.

We arrive at the first vineyard at 5:30 A.M. A crew of
workers is picking grapes near the road. Alongside the road
are scattered empty crates with the label: Coachella Valley
Grapes. A rancher drives to the scene in his Cadillac and
parks it between the workers and the approaching pickets.
It is equipped with air-conditioning and a two-way radio.
On the bumper of his car is a sign that reads: *Eat California
Grapes, the Forbidden Fruit!*

The strikers park their cars and carry their picket signs
to the edge of the vineyards. The signs read: *Huelga, Coachella,* "No Contract, No Work!" "We Want Justice! We
Want Contracts!" *Justicia a los Campesinos!* (Justice for
Farm Workers!) *Viva la Huelga!*

The symbol of the black eagle is everywhere—on the picket signs, on flags, on the shirts, hats, and armbands of the pickets, and on the bumper stickers of the strikers' jalopies. It is said that the black eagle is a symbol of the Mexican people, bequeathed to them by their Aztec forebears. Cesar's brother Manuel squared off the edges of the eagle, so that farm workers could easily duplicate the image.

A pickup truck with a camper and Texas license plates creates a wake of dust as it comes to a stop on the soft shoulder of the road. On the back of the truck is inscribed: "Osvaldo Chapas, Brownsville, Texas." The Chapases are one of the more than eighty migratory worker families who walked out on strike from Valley Vista Farms yesterday. Today Osvaldo is carrying a *huelga* flag and his four daughters are carrying picket signs. They are all pretty, dark skinned, and in their late teens. They are dressed as they were yesterday when they walked out of the fields—in slacks and sweat shirts. They protect their heads from the dust and sweat in the vineyards by wearing bandanas and wide-brimmed straw hats. Like most migrant families, the Chapases are Roman Catholics. A crucifix and a small statue of Our Lady of Guadalupe adorn the cab of their father's pickup. On the front bumper, a sign reads: *Dios Es Amor* (God Is Love). They join the picket line. They shout to the pickers, *"Venganse, hermanos y hermanas! Huelga! Huelga! Huelga!"* (Come on out, brothers and sisters! Strike! Strike! Strike!)

Maria Lucia Almazan is calling out to two of her friends in the field. Maria is forty-five years old and walked out on strike yesterday. For the past few years, she has been supporting her seventy-seven-year-old mother in Texas. If she had worked hard during the harvest season, Maria could have sent her mother $100 a month. But she has chosen to go out on strike to help build a better future for countless thousands of workers and their families. Maria was insulted when she left the field yesterday. Her crew boss called her a dirty double-crossing Mexican. She tried to hide the tears when I saw her come out. Some of the women strikers had embraced her at the entrance to the vineyard.

During the latter part of the morning, an olive-drab-colored car with the words "California State Department of Employment" drives slowly by the picket line. A few of the pickets shout *Huelga!* at the four Anglos in the car. Another picket shouts in Spanish, *"Huelga,* puppets of the growers!" Several other pickets make angry remarks as the car parks some distance away from the picket line. The California Department of Employment has a very shady history indeed, regarding farm labor. Ernesto Galarza details some of its worst moments in his book *Merchants of Labor.* The department has been notorious for helping growers to break strikes and for recruiting foreign labor to depress domestic wage scales for decades. It will apparently, under the Reagan Administration, do everything in its power to help break the strike this season.

Seventeen-year-old José Uribe, Jr., has also joined the picket line. He mentions to me that he works evenings at a resort in nearby Palm Desert. One of the farm owners whose vineyard had been picketed yesterday had come in late last night. He had drunk himself to sleep at the bar. José winced with disgust as he told me how the growers so often treat their workers with contempt. Later on, José, Sr., told me of his experiences as a cook in one of the elegant resort hotels in Palm Springs—only a half-hour drive from Coachella. He recounted how the rich throw their money away on trivia and complain ceaselessly about the exquisite food, while, a few short miles away, farm workers who provide this food live and work in virtual slavery. I immediately recalled what a worker had told me a few weeks earlier in the Imperial Valley town of Brawley. He said that he thought the workers who immigrate from Mexico on temporary visas are more enslaved than the blacks who were bought at auction blocks in the South 200 years ago. This man observed that at least a slave was an investment that had to be handled with a certain amount of care. But, if a Mexican worker contracts some serious disease or breaks an arm or a leg, his employer will simply ship him back to Mexico and get another man the next day. Under the *bracero* program, this traffic in human flesh had the force of law: Public Law 78. The program tolerated horrifying conditions reminiscent of wartime concentration camps.

As the sun rises over the valley, the temperature soars. By 10 A.M., it is already 105 degrees. It will be 110 today. It will stay that way until at least 6:30 in the evening.

A young mother pours a cup of cold water for her small boy from the back of a pickup truck. Meanwhile, picket captain Robert Bustos approaches UFWOC attorney Frank Dennison. Robert had just entered a nearby field to speak to the workers. He was spotted by a foreman who immediately called the ranch owner to the scene. The owner ordered the foreman to seize Bustos until the sheriff's deputies arrived. When the lawmen appeared, they advised the rancher that he had no right to seize anyone on his property unless they first refused to leave. Attorney Dennison takes an affidavit from Bustos and tells him he has a case for false arrest. On the day before, a special investigator, paid by the growers, had seized a young girl named Beatrice Sanchez in another vineyard. He had not asked her any questions. It was very difficult to control the picket line when the strikers had seen what had taken place. It was even more difficult to restrain the strikers when they saw another rancher brutally attack picket captain Tony Lopez only a few feet from the picket line. The strikers were also very disturbed that Bill Lester, the local constable, was fraternizing with the growers and joking about the picket line. He had asked the Riverside County Board of Supervisors for a shotgun rack and a supply of chemical Mace just before the strike started. His permission was denied.

More Mexican-American students have joined us on the picket line. One of them, Miguel Becerra, is from Brawley.

He tells me, "Did you know that it was not until after the war that Mexicans were able to participate in athletics in Brawley? And it wasn't until the early 1950's that the local swimming pool was integrated—Mexicans and Anglos?" Miguel joined the strikers who were engaging in conversations with the strikebreakers. He has fully identified with the cause of his people and sports a Zapatista mustache. A button on his shirt shows a picture of Emiliano Zapata, the Mexican revolutionary, with the caption, *Nosotros Venceremos*. Miguel points out that several of his fellow high school students were just expelled for wearing this button to class. They were now fighting the expulsion in a superior court in San Diego.

Across from the picket line, three growers discuss the strike. One of them makes remarks about a sign carried by one of the pickets. The sign reads, "Negotiate!" The rancher grins and shouts to two Filipino pickets, "Negotiate what? My workers are happy!"

One of the Filipinos wipes the sweat from his brow and begins to speak through a loudspeaker. His name is Felicin Ytom, a striker from Delano. He addresses himself to his Filipino brothers, speaking in Tagalog and English. He asks them to come out on strike. He reminds them of the former strikes they had made together. He speaks of the mutual suffering and exploitation they had undergone at the hands of the growers. "Come on, our brothers, join the struggle," he says. "Don't be a slave all of your lives. I am appealing to you as your brother. Fight for a guaranteed wage! Fight for your rights! Come on out and join your brothers!"

Felicin did not go into detail about the strike the Filipinos had in Coachella in 1965. He did not say how the men were mercilessly harassed by the growers. The gas, electricity, and water was cut off at the camps. When the men returned from the fields they found their clothing and belongings thrown into the dirt yards near the vineyards. This had been their reward for the years of toil they had given to the grape growers in the valley. Felicin puts the microphone down, grabs a picket sign, and looks across the vines to where his brothers pack the grapes. His hope is that they will eventually come out and look for work elsewhere. The rumor has it that many of them will be leaving in the next few days.

On the evening of June 16, at the peak of the grape harvest, three Filipino farm workers were arrested at Bagdasarian Camp Number Two. It was midnight—the only illumination available came from the headlights of the strikers' jalopies. The lights, electricity, and water had been shut off. Over 100 strikers gathered in prayer, as the three men were led to the sheriff's automobiles and from there to the Riverside County Jail in Indio.

Earlier that day, thirty farm workers had been evicted from the camp. They had been on strike for the last six days against Bagdasarian Farms and its general manager, Mike Bozick. They were testing a previous ruling, which stated that a worker in the state of California may not be evicted from his home for thirty days should he go on strike. They were also telling Bozick that his messages to the press were wrong—they were not *his happy workers,* and they *did* want a union.

Before the arrests were made, we held a religious service. The strikers, Filipino single men, Chicano farm workers and students, attorneys, and volunteers gathered around the three men.

It was another of the many "liturgies of protest" we held during the strike. The last one was held in the David Freedman Corporation camp. It was a memorial service for Robert F. Kennedy on the anniversary of his tragic death. A delegation of Canadian United Auto Workers, headed by Dennis MacDermott, accompanied us. Toward the end of the service, a sheriff's deputy asked us to leave. We had dispersed, singing *Nosotros Venceremos.*

Any workers' barracks in the Coachella Valley, with its "No Trespassing" signs and concentration-camp appearance, is a powerful symbol of human bondage. It tells the tragic story of the past 100 years of California agriculture. A feudal system of owners, bosses, labor contractors, fore-

men, and workers built an agricultural empire. John
Steinbeck had stated, referring to the Filipinos, "The history of California's importation and treatment of foreign
labor is a disgraceful picture of greed and cruelty." The
unpardonable sin of the Filipino farm workers was their
tendency to organize for their own protection.

The three workers arrested were: Elias Banequed, a
sixty-five-year-old foreman, and two eighteen-year-olds, Fer-
nando Abalos and Bill Denman. They were arrested at
midnight after the brief service, charged with trespassing
and contempt of a court order that demanded they leave
the property. After the arrests, eviction notices were tacked
to the doors of bunkhouses, forbidding anyone from enter-
ing the building.

The next day, Mike Bozick appeared on the edge of a
Bagdasarian vineyard and told Richard Chavez, a brother
of Cesar, that he would die before he ever signed a union
contract. (One year later, and very much alive, Bozick
signed.) The short man tugged at his panama hat, puffed
nervously on his cigar, then disappeared in a cloud of dust
in his air-conditioned ranch wagon. He would keep contact
with his foremen in the fields by means of his two-way
radio. Among farm workers, Bozick's code name is Mr.
Bagdad Grape. Agitation and fear were clearly manifested
in his face. His own workers were now challenging him
fearlessly. His worry was compounded by the fact that ten
other growers had agreed to begin negotiations with the
union.

Meanwhile, a strong desert wind blew through the Coachella Valley and the Bagdasarian camp. The camp was
abandoned. Its silence was a memorial to the men who had
stood up against an unjust system. They knew, however,
that the next time they worked for Mr. Bagdad Grape it
would be under a union contract.

The afternoon sun gets oppressively hot in July as the
harvest season comes to an end in the Coachella Valley. By
this time most of the grapes are already on display in super-

markets throughout the country. Many of the housewives shopping in air-conditioned comfort had never heard about Pete Velasco or Maria Lucia Almazan or the Chapas family. They had probably never seen a migratory worker from Texas or known about the sad plight of Filipinos in the fields of California. But somehow the message of the strike reached them, and grape sales declined.

The long hot days on the picket line were not spent in vain. The Coachella growers knew that it was only a matter of time before they carried the black eagle on their grape boxes. The grape growers in Delano were also beginning to face reality. Cesar jokingly told a group of volunteers that the new catch-phrase was, "Boycott, Baby, Boycott!"

[8]

The Grape Boycott: A Success Story

The international boycott of table grapes was a success story without parallel in the history of American labor. The walls of resistance came tumbling down in spring, 1970, when the first collective-bargaining agreements were signed with the table-grape industry.

The fact that the initial pacts were signed in one of the offices of the Archdiocese of Los Angeles in the presence of Roman Catholic bishops is significant.

It was the first time in the history of the church in the United States that the Roman Catholic hierarchy had taken such a direct role in a major labor dispute. The bishops' farm-labor committee was intended to be an ad hoc group but became a permanent entity after the first contracts were signed. Its effectiveness was and is proof that the institutional church can make meaningful contributions to contemporary social problems.

Just before the breakthrough with the grape growers,

UFWOC discovered a dramatic drop in the demand for table grapes in major U.S. cities. Large quantities of unsold grapes were dumped into the wine market at a loss to growers. Surplus grapes were sold to fruit vendors in Mexico at giveaway prices. Retailers, who formerly bought and paid for grapes in advance, bought them only on consignment in the final months of the boycott. This meant lower prices. Hundreds of car lots were returned to California unsold.

Boycott rallies, demonstrations, and marches became commonplace in mid-1968 throughout the United States. Although the grape industry undertook a costly publicity campaign, it was impossible to counteract the dramatic message of the boycotters, most of whom had spent their lives in the vineyards in Kern and Tulare counties. They spoke convincingly at every gathering that would listen to them, from women's church sodalities to meetings of the Black Panthers.

During the Presidential race of 1968, Senators Robert F. Kennedy, Eugene McCarthy, and George McGovern endorsed the boycott along with Vice-President Hubert H. Humphrey, while Governor Ronald Reagan of California and Richard Nixon denounced it and ate grapes at a press conference in Fresno.

Grapes were served with fanfare at fund-raising dinners for the U.S. Senatorial campaign of conservative Max Rafferty in California. They also decorated the tables at the inaugural banquet of Vice-President Spiro Agnew.

Since August, 1967, UFWOC had been striking and boycotting Giumarra Vineyards Corporation near Bakersfield, whose 12,000 acres constitute the largest table-grape holdings in the world. In order to break the boycott, Giumarra began to use the labels of other growers on its own grape boxes. By the end of 1967, it was using 105 different labels. When other grape growers refused to discuss recognition procedures with the union, the boycott was extended to cover all California grapes.

Boycott volunteers and full-time strikers were sent out
to preach the boycott to anybody who would listen. A boycott rally, complete with Hollywood stars, took place in
downtown Los Angeles; penitential fasts by seminarians
were held in front of A & P stores on Long Island and in
Philadelphia; a sit-in confronted the headquarters of the
Jewel Tea Corporation in Chicago. Thirty-five people,
including a nun and a priest, were arrested in a sit-in at
the headquarters of Safeway stores, in Oakland, California.

Meanwhile, growers both condemned the boycott and
denied it was having any effect. Delano grape grower Jack
Pandol called the boycott "unmoral, illegal, unChristian,
and un-American." Pandol is a leader of the Knights of
Columbus and the Californians for Right-to-Work Laws.

In February, 1969, dockers in London, England, refused
to unload any more than 70,000 pounds of grapes. Further-
more, the European Transport and General Workers
Union endorsed the boycott, and the Swedish Transport
Workers also rallied to the cause, causing a grape blockade
in Northern Europe.

Late in April, 1969, California growers launched a
multi-million-dollar public-relations campaign to counter
the boycott. They hired two public-relations firms,
Whittaker and Baxter of San Francisco and J. Walter
Thompson of New York.

On June 15, 1969, a maverick group of ten grape growers
who had been hard hit by the boycott began to negotiate
with the farm workers' union. One of the growers, Lionel
Steinberg, of Coachella, admitted that the production cost
of grapes that year, $5.50 a lug, was the same as the price at
the market place. The previous year the market price had
been $10 a lug.

The Delano grape growers resented the move of the ten
growers and retaliated with a press conference on June 16.
Spokesman Martin Zaninovich announced that they
"would not sell out the American consumer or the farm
workers by yielding to the demands of the United Farm

Workers Organizing Committee. . . . This industry, as long as it must, will fight Chavez, whose policy is an outrage to decency in what we loosely call a civilized era."

Meanwhile, other grape growers filed a $75 million suit in a federal court in Fresno for damages caused by the boycott. The suit also demanded an injunction to outlaw the grape boycott. The suit is still pending and may be pursued during the coming harvest season.

UFWOC attorneys claimed that consumer boycotts were protected by the First Amendment. They also said that secondary boycotts are not illegal for farm workers, because they have never been covered by the National Labor Relations Act (NLRA).

As the boycott became successful, grower publications such as the *California Farmer* recorded the drop in prices and called upon their readers to give financial support to the public-relations firm Whittaker and Baxter. They also rallied to aid the "Consumer's Rights Bill" of Senator George Murphy, a California Republican, which would outlaw boycotts and strikes at harvest time in agriculture.

Cesar felt that the Murphy bill was repressive. "Its only intent is to destroy the farm workers' rights and aspirations to form a strong union," he said. Cesar wants the protective provisions of the Wagner Act without the Taft-Hartley and Landrum-Griffin amendments, which prohibit secondary boycotting and limit strike activities. In other words, he asks that the NLRA be revised to protect the organization of farm workers during the early critical years of their union.

It is estimated that between $7 million and $10 million had been paid to Whittaker and Baxter to fight the boycott. The same firm helped defeat President Truman's national health-insurance program in 1948 and told the American public in 1964, about Barry Goldwater, that "In your heart, you know he's right."

The firm had a staff of twenty-five people operating out of New York, Washington, D.C., and Chicago telling the public the growers' version of the grape strike. It also sponsored all-expense-paid tours of the Delano vineyards for community leaders throughout the nation and Canada. The chief aim was to change the issue from "worker rights" to "consumer rights," from bargaining rights of farm workers to buying rights of housewives.

The basic issue in the grape strike and boycott was the right of workers to bargain collectively with their employers for decent wages and working conditions. Farm workers were denied the protection of the law during the 1930's, when other industrial workers were covered by the National Labor Relations Act.

The genius of the Chavez movement was that it was run along the lines of a community organization based on full participation of the striking families.

Growers remained firmly entrenched against unions in agriculture. Their chief complaint was against the boycott, which they claimed was immoral. They stated that California farm workers received the highest wages of any of the nation's farm hands. They added that their workers were adequately protected by health, sanitation, child labor, and housing laws. They took vigorous exception to the introduction of the pesticide issue, which they believed was a last-ditch attempt by Chavez to mislead the public and wreak havoc among growers.

Industry spokesmen, backed by Governor Reagan and Senator George Murphy, continuously asserted that "Chavez is not out to organize farm workers, but to control all agriculture, to rule or ruin the industry."

Here, in summary, was the growers' position:

California farm workers do not want to be represented by Chavez's union. Farm workers around Delano are longtime residents and not migrants, as they are described by union spokesmen. The real farm workers have never been on strike; in fact, there has never been a true strike.

Chavez is a social revolutionary and not a labor organizer. He speaks of such issues as race and nonviolence and the denial of civil rights to black and brown farm workers by the police, the courts, and the local governments in the towns of the Southwest.

Moreover, growers do not have the financial resources to withstand unionization. Paying union wages will be the straw that breaks the camel's back.

At best, Chavez is a power-hungry opportunist, who is amassing a small fortune from the dues of the workers and the contributions of do-gooders. All he is able to offer in return are empty promises.

Mrs. Dolores Huerta, a vice-president of UFWOC, agrees that there are many laws designed to protect the health and safety of the workers on the job. But, she maintains, "the only way to get these laws enforced is through a union contract. Only through collective-bargaining agreements can both the worker and the consumer be safeguarded against pesticide poisoning. Even if laws are passed concerning the use of pesticides, who will enforce them?"

It was the farm workers' union that was largely responsible for alerting the public to the menace of DDT use as an agricultural pesticide. This led to a widespread ban on the poison. Because of the pressure of UFWOC, the California State Department of Public Health conducted a survey on farm workers in Tulare County. The results showed that 80 per cent of the workers interviewed had suffered adverse effects because of their contacts with the poisons. The collective-bargaining agreements with the vineyards prohibit the use of DDT, DDD, Aldrin Dieldrin, and Endrin. They also stipulate that a committee elected by the workers control the application of pesticides and that no worker enter a field where parathion has been applied for twenty-one days.

The growers' claim that farm workers in the Delano area were mostly local residents has been disputed in a 1968 study by Richard Fineberg, *Green Card Labor and the Delano Grape Strike,* prepared for the Council for Christian Social Action of the United Church of Christ.

Fineberg found that of the 7,000 harvest workers in Delano, only 32 per cent lived and worked in the vicinity the year round.

To the charge that farm workers did not want to be represented by Chavez, UFWOC pointed out that it had won every valid election and card check it conducted.

Phillip Veracruz, another UFWOC vice-president, stated that the grapes were harvested by workers the growers recruited from South Texas and Mexico. "The growers even put ads in Mexican newspapers as far away as Juarez, Mexico. There are laws against aliens breaking our strike, but the immigration authorities just look the other way."

Chavez bitterly complained that the U.S. Justice Department has done nothing to prevent alien strikebreaking, even though UFWOC supplied abundant information that it was taking place in 1968 and 1969. In his October, 1969, testimony before Congress, Chavez said:

There are thousands of alien workers and illegal entries which make up the work force on 90 per cent of the struck ranches. The congressmen present already know how effective the border patrol can be when it wants to stop marijuana from being imported into the country. It is obvious that human beings used as strikebreakers could be stopped even more easily than the weed. It is difficult for the farm worker to have faith in his government when it is *de facto* involved in strikebreaking activities.

His crisis of belief is not lessened when he discovered that the Defense Department has been instrumental in giving direct aid to the struck growers. The DOD has increased its shipments of grapes to South Vietnam by 800 per cent since the strike began in 1965. South Vietnam now ranks No. 3 in foreign grape exports.

Chavez also claimed that racism is common in California agriculture. He asserted that the best jobs are given to Anglos, that the Delano growers have kept Mexicans, blacks, Filipinos, Puerto Ricans, and Arabs in separate labor camps, and that pitting one group against another has been a common practice.

The size of the vineyard corporations is frequently cited as an issue in the strike and boycott. Congressman B. F. Sisk, Democrat of Fresno, has opposed the boycott, claiming that it was directed against the small growers, who, he said, made up the majority.

UFWOC denied that this was true, citing figures from the U.S. Census of Agriculture, showing that 7 per cent of California farms own 75 per cent of the land. The union also says that the average size of the vineyards around Delano is over 2,000 acres. According to the University of California publication *The Economic Review of the California Grape Industry,* "The fresh grape industry is centered around 30 shippers. Approximately 85 per cent of all table grapes is handled by these thirty growers." The Giumarra Vineyards Corporation, which UFWOC struck in 1967, ships 2,000 car lots of grapes each year—10 per cent of all table-grape shipments.

The boycott was also an all-out confrontation against the most powerful allies that agribusiness has—the chain-store supermarkets. Although the markets claimed neutrality during the dispute, they sided with the growers against the workers. Samuel Johnson, Executive Director of the San Francisco Bay Area Grocers Association, proudly stated that the markets were "fighting the battle for the farmers." Safeway bought over $4 million worth of struck grapes in 1969.

But the consumers, throughout the United States and Canada, refrained from buying grapes. Boycott organizers such as Marcos Muñoz went directly to the suburbs and appealed to the consumers. "We knew that the people who buy the grapes live in the suburbs," Marcos said. "So we began to have house meetings around Boston. We brought people together who lived on the same block but never knew each other. Area coordinators were appointed. Others would check the stores and distribute leaflets. These people helped us clear the scab grapes off the shelves," he added.

The boycott organizers would show the film *Decision in Delano* and tell their audiences that farm workers received less than $2,000 a year for their labor. They quoted the Governor's Advisory Committee on Housing Problems, which stated that "the farm worker remains among the most poorly paid, poorly fed, and poorly housed of California's citizens. Four out of every five farm workers live in substandard dwellings. One out of every four lacks even running water." Farm workers have the highest occupational disease rate in California. Death rates among infants of farm workers are higher than those of any other occupational group. Their children are still excluded from child-labor and school-attendance laws.

In addition to an AFL-CIO-affiliated union, Chavez also provides farm workers and the nonworking poor with a service center, composed of a credit union, a co-op filling station, a clinic, and a retirement village for elderly Filipino workers. Staff workers at the center assist workers with translation services for immigration papers, income tax forms, and workmen's compensation and disability cases. They also intercede for workers at the courts and welfare departments, and with the police. Cesar has elaborate plans for the co-op and service-center aspects of his organization but has been forced to direct full attention to the struggles with the agricultural industry. He feels that the poor must build their own economic institutions in order to survive in American society.

After the majority of the table-grape growers had signed contracts with UFWOC, the enormous task of enforcing the pacts and of educating workers began. Added to this was the new conflict with the lettuce industry. Within the space of two years, the farm workers' union had grown from a position of insecurity to one of power.

"Our job now is to consolidate our gains," Cesar said.

Shortly after he made this statement, he discovered that the Western Conference of Teamsters had begun to organize field workers throughout California. After the lettuce strike reached its peak, Cesar made plans to tour the United States again, this time to seek support for the lettuce boycott.

He was to stress nonviolence as the only worthwhile method of achieving real social change. "Nonviolence," he said, "means that masses of people come to the aid of their less fortunate brothers who are legally, legitimately, and nonviolently trying to get a better life for themselves and their families."

[9]

James Caswell: A Hero for California's Rural Poor

Leaders from among the poor and oppressed have been telling us that the problems of the poor are problems that the poor did not originate; rather, the poor are the victims of injustices perpetrated by businessmen and the so-called silent majority of middle-class America.

It is refreshing to see men like Jim Caswell use his power and prestige as a businessman to serve the poor. Jim had no formal training as an organizer. He had no particular ideological ax to grind. He was not "agitating the Mexicans," as his opponents charged. He was affirming a common brotherhood he had with all men, rich as well as poor. A *Los Angeles Times* article called him a mystery man. It is indeed sad that, when a man chooses to help his brothers and fight injustice, standing up for authentic human values, he is misunderstood or condemned.

Unfortunately, there are few James Caswells in this world. Jim's story is still relatively unknown. Perhaps the few words in this chapter will advance his cause, as well as serve to encourage the many liberals who believe that they cannot do much to change the face of America.

I met Jim Caswell only once. It was during the Coachella Valley Grape Strike in the summer of 1968. Everyone seemed to notice Jim; some for his immense physical size—over 300 pounds, others because of his friendly manner and good reputation among the poor of the valley.

Mexican-American farm workers, welfare mothers, indigent students, and prison inmates admired him without limit. But community leaders and officials in the Coachella Valley considered Jim a troublemaker and a professional radical who came to town "to stir up the Mexicans."

Caswell was a Canadian by birth. He studied at the University of California at Berkeley, built up a successful reputation as a businessman, and was twice divorced before arriving in the Coachella Valley.

His doctors had told him that the dry, hot climate would help him cope with his chronic asthma. Coachella Valley, best known for the wealthy resort town of Palm Springs, was converted into a verdant garden from desert wastes only thirty years ago. The desert yielded lush vineyards and rich groves of citrus and dates when its soil absorbed the cool waters of the Colorado River.

Few people admit that the valley would still be a wasteland if it were not for the back-breaking labor of the migratory workers imported to plant and harvest the diversified crops of the area. These were the dust-bowlers that Woody Guthrie sang about and the Mexicans and Filipinos that John Steinbeck described as "needed but hated." Their homes are now weather-beaten shacks and time-worn labor camps that hug the outskirts of the valley towns of Indio, Coachella, Thermal, and Mecca.

During the war years, farm work was done by labor from

Mexico under the *bracero* program. In recent years, entire families have immigrated from Mexico to do this work. These newcomers are called green-carders, because of the color of their visas. Substandard wages, language barriers, and racial discrimination hold these people in a state of virtual bondage, creating a myriad of social problems.

Caswell arrived in the valley in 1960. Two of his closest friends, Raul Loya and Miguel Figueroa, traced his activities for me one afternoon in an Indio coffee shop.

Loya, an activist in the Mexican-American Political Association (MAPA) lost his job as a high school teacher because of his involvement with Caswell in controversial community issues. He spoke intensely and reverently about Caswell. "Jim began to understand the power structure in the valley. His interest in the young Chicanos became widely known, and he was invited to look into the problem of recruiting more of them into the College of the Desert by the school administration. His findings were an indictment of the power structure in the valley. Jim couldn't believe his own carefully gathered facts: A large percentage of the kids could hardly read or write English. Jim spent days and months talking to the kids about their problems. He then formed a committee to study the problems further. The committee became very critical of the board of education and other officials. Some of the teachers who served on the committee met with constant harassment from conservative elements in the community. They resigned because of the intimidation, but Jim fought on."

Miguel Figueroa, who wears a Zapatista mustache, is also active in MAPA. "Jim was always after the students to continue their education," he said. "He helped several students enter local colleges, and a few were accepted into the University of California."

Loya broke into the conversation: "Jim was all heart! He was out to help people. Without him, nothing would have ever happened in the Coachella Valley. He knew the issues and the problems. Yet he still couldn't believe his eyes. He couldn't believe that the Mexican Americans were being oppressed to such a degree. We used to tell him, 'Jim, for crying out loud, every time we turn around they oppress us. Only twenty years ago they were still hanging us!' "

"There was always the undercurrent among the city officials and growers that Jim was a communist," Figueroa added. " 'Where does he get his finances?' they asked. 'What's he really up to?' "

"He spent a lot of his energy on the farm-labor problem," Loya said. "By this time, he had depleted his own personal savings and got a job as a bill-collector. When Willard Wirtz, the Secretary of Labor under the Johnson Administration, came to the valley with an investigating committee, Jim set up a meeting. The farmers were showing Wirtz only the best labor camps. Jim arranged a special tour and showed them all the camps.

"This really set the power structure against Jim. Then, when farm-labor leader Cesar Chavez and his union organizers needed help during the strike against Di Giorgio Farms at Borrego Springs in 1966, Jim was right there. He donated rooms for the organizers when they passed through Indio. He filled their tanks with gas, so they could get to the vineyards at Borrego.

"When Chavez came to Coachella to begin the grape strike in 1968, Jim furnished an office, telephones, and living quarters for the organizers. Two months later, Jim was fired by his employer, a collection-agency executive, allegedly because of his connection with the union.

"Jim was working for the poor twenty-four hours a day. If it wasn't farm workers, it would be students, welfare, poverty programs, political campaigns, and elections. He couldn't stand injustice in any form. His heart went out to everyone."

Caswell's other activities included expanding MAPA membership from ten to seventy-five, building a large Democratic precinct organization, and running for the

Indio City Council and the Economic Opportunities Board of Commissioners. Jim lost the former position but won a seat on the EOC. He was appalled at the obstacle course the poor encountered when they sought to break the chains of their poverty. He was further depressed at the right-wing political mood of the valley. The elected officials looked upon the provisions of the Economic Opportunity Act as fostering "organized insurrection." What else, they thought, could "maximum feasible participation of the poor" mean?

In May, 1965, Caswell was elected a member of the Policy Commission for the Economic Opportunity Programs in Riverside County. His election caused an uproar among the conservatives in the valley, who felt that he was an outsider and did not represent, according to a Coachella newspaper, "the stable, clear thinking people of the area."

During his tenure as commissioner, Caswell proposed a "Community Developers Project." It was designed to train approximately fifteen Mexican-American youths as community organizers. One of the students most interested in the project was Henry Perez, a slightly built, serious youth. Caswell later helped him to enter the Loyola University Law School in Los Angeles. Caswell submitted the proposal on the project several times. Each time, it was rejected by the majority of the commissioners. One of the board members later stated, "Actually, the project was okay in its final form; but its leadership [Caswell] was too controversial, so we had to turn it down."

The project failed, but it cemented Caswell's relationships with an important segment of the valley's poor, the young people. The conservatives in the valley were not about to sanction a program that had for its aims: "Motivating young people with personal roots in poverty to pursue college education in professions that make them valuable in Community Action programs."

When Chavez's union prepared to strike the vineyards in the Coachella Valley in May, 1968, Caswell made several attempts to reconcile community leaders and growers to the farm-union movement. He and Raul Loya released the following statement to the press during the 1968 Coachella grape strike:

> The citizens, merchants, police departments, city council members and local newspapers should reflect on their stand concerning Cesar Chavez and his farm workers union. . . . The *Coachella Valley Sun* took a propaganda position supporting the farmers, publishing a John Birch Society petition to deny the union the use of public facilities.
>
> The police department has repeatedly issued citations to the cars of the grape strikers, and local organizations, including the Catholic Church, have denied the union the use of their facilities for meetings.
>
> We suggest that the merchants and their friends visit Delano, where hatred has grown to unbelievable proportions since the strike began. . . . We do not want to see this happen in Coachella. . . . We should use our influence to get the *Coachella Valley Sun* to print both sides of the story and stop the city officials and police from discriminating, intimidating, and harassing the strikers.

Caswell's chief opponent was Gale Ellis, conservative editor of the *Coachella Valley Sun* and president of the Coachella Chamber of Commerce. Ellis directed several editorial potshots at Caswell and Loya, calling them "threatening agitators." The two retaliated, leading a group of pickets on the offices of the *Sun*. Their picket signs read: "Gale Ellis is prejudiced," "The *C V Sun* is Sour Grapes," and "Don't Buy the *C V Sun*."

On July 4, 1968, Democratic Congressman John Tunney from the 38th District and now U.S. Senator since his 1970 victory over George Murphy, spoke at a rally in Coachella. Tunney, in his mid-thirties, is the son of the famous prize fighter. He tells of being a roommate with Senator Ted Kennedy at the University of Virginia Law School. The young politician (with a somewhat contrived

Kennedy look) was then running for re-election in his district, which includes Riverside and Imperial counties. He chose Coachella, the heart of the grape and citrus country, to appeal to the rural Mexican-American vote.

Chavez supporters, led by Caswell and Loya, were angered by his refusal to support the grape boycott. Tunney considered the boycott a labor-management problem and not a political issue. When he began to speak about farm-labor problems, omitting any mention of Chavez or the boycott, Alfredo Figueroa, Miguel's brother, raised a large banner with the union's black eagle insignia. Union supporters began to clap and cheer, allegedly drowning out Tunney's 4th of July rhetoric for five minutes.

Just before the rally began, Caswell and Loya called off a picket line designed to embarrass Tunney, at the latter's request. Tunney offered to meet with the dissidents at the nearby Thunderbird Motel after the rally. According to Tom Kay, a young union volunteer from Michigan, "Tunney hemmed and hawed at the meeting, holding fast to his original position. Everyone except Loya and Caswell walked out on him."

Five of the alleged clap-down participants were singled out in complaints for conspiring to disturb the peace, filed two weeks later by the Coachella Police Department. The complaints were issued through the office of the district attorney at the request of the city of Coachella. The five were: James Caswell, Raul Loya, Tom Kay, Alberto Figueroa, and Ramses Noriego, a student from UCLA.

Tunney was heavily criticized by Chicano leaders for doing nothing to prevent the arrests. He said that he had publicly defended the right of the demonstrators to dissent. "All we know," Loya said, "is that, two weeks later, the warrants for our arrest were issued. The point is *not* that Tunney put the finger on us. The point is that he could have stopped the charges, and he didn't."

Right up to the last moment, Jim denied clapping at the rally. He told me this many times.

"The cards were stacked against us at the trial," Loya continued. "The judge . . . has always been against minority groups. He has treated Mexicans like animals for years. How could we get a fair shake at the trial? The whole thing was a conspiracy against us as far as I'm concerned."

Tom Kay, one of the defendants, was reached by phone in Detroit. "The whole trial was a farce," he said. "Alfredo Figueroa could not possibly have been clapping. He had a heavy banner in his hands. It was six feet tall with an awkward cross section. Nor did anyone have evidence on Caswell. Jim could hardly keep from laughing at the trial when the townspeople pointed the finger at him. He never believed he would be sent to jail. All of us were buoyant during the trial. We joked about the people on the witness stand. They were obviously molding the truth to their own advantage. It was clearly a conspiracy to silence two political activists—Loya and Caswell. The rest of us were taken along for the ride."

On August 30, 1968, a guilty sentence was handed to Caswell, Loya, Kay, and Figueroa. Charges against Noriega were dropped. Although their attorney had stated in their defense that they had followed, in their noise and clapping, U.S. political tradition, "which was rude, but not criminal," the four received 120-day jail sentences. The four men began serving their time, after several appeals and delays, in June, 1969.

Caswell was concerned that Tom Kay receive medication for his epilepsy while in prison. Upon his release, Caswell dictated his prison memories to Henry Perez at the latter's home in Venice, California. Perez did not tell me why Caswell wanted the facts in writing, but it seemed in keeping with his passion for justice to have all the facts straight.

The hand-written text began: ". . . . Upon our arrival in Riverside, Kay told them at the front desk that he was supposed to receive medicine four times a day. They merely grabbed it and said that he would get it twice a day there. . . . I continued to get my medicine, but they did not give Kay his. He got very upset. Then, on Sunday afternoon, a number of people rushed into the dispensary for a stretcher saying that someone had suffered a heart attack. I asked them if it was Tom Kay, and they said it was. I told them that it must have been an epileptic seizure. Kay told me later that they only gave him one mild pill. About twelve midnight, the next night, they rushed into the dispensary again—Kay had another seizure. This time he had fallen off a top bunk, opening two gashes on his forehead. They called for an ambulance and took him to the Riverside County Hospital."

Caswell dictated that he was continually given the wrong medicine at the wrong time for his own ailments. "I developed several pus blisters on my feet, but they wouldn't give me any socks," Caswell narrated. "My right leg began to swell."

"I could not walk on the leg," Caswell related. "Other prisoners brought my food a couple of times. But the jailer stopped this and insisted that I get in line like everyone else or he would put me in the drunk tank. I was simply not able to do it, so he forced me to hop along on my right foot to the drunk tank. I was kept there the entire day."

"Jim seemed incredibly naïve to us," Loya said. "We were brought up in the barrios. You can't live there and not have a run-in with the cops now and then. But Jim Caswell was really innocent. He used to feel sorry for the guys that were intimidated in jail or made fun of by the other prisoners. I'll never forget an old man that was so drunk he couldn't work a water fountain. The others made fun of him. But Jim walked over and helped him. I remember that some guys were making noise at night, and Jim told them to be quiet. It took me the longest time to explain to him that one doesn't do that kind of a thing in jail. People have a way of taking revenge there. It's the law of the jungle.

"Jim couldn't believe the things that were going on in jail—the weird relationships, the homosexuality, the subsociety and its harsh atmosphere. Somehow he had been protected from these things all his life. Most of all, he couldn't believe he was actually in jail. It seemed like a bad dream to him. After a month in jail, Jim lost a lot of weight. He was not his old self. The experience was traumatic for him, and he never got over it."

Kay also recalled Caswell's interest in the other prisoners. "Jim would spend hours with Alfred Figueroa in the Indio jail talking to Mexican aliens who had entered the U.S. illegally and were awaiting deportation. Jim would offer suggestions to help the men locate their families. He also helped an inmate file a suit against the county for some indignities incurred while he was in jail. It was beautiful to see Jim with people."

Kay noticed the deterioration of Caswell's health while in prison. "We could see Jim failing every day. He was promised several doctors who never came. He began to lie down a lot. He was always weak and tired and sweating. When he finally got his medicine, it was too late to do him any good."

After the four were released, Alfredo Figueroa issued the following statement:

Prior to our arrival at the facility [Riverside County Jail] a riot had taken place. There were complaints about food, police brutality, and sanitation. This kind of incarceration made it impossible for Jim to retain his mental and physical health while in prison. At the time of his discharge, he was brought in a nonambulatory condition to a local hospital. . . . We are seeking action to remedy the conditions at the Riverside County Jail and are willing to proceed with all legal action to bring about an end to these conditions.

Raul Loya remarked that the prison experience left permanent scars on James Caswell. He was up and around for a while after his release but soon lapsed into morbid depressions and a series of physical ailments that led to his death in a Riverside hospital on November 19, 1969, four months after he was released from prison.

The Caswell funeral took place on the outskirts of the small town of Coachella on November 24. The Reverend James Drake and I were invited to participate in the burial services. Drake is a member of the California Migrant Ministry and Cesar Chavez's administrative assistant. Since we had been involved in the grape strike in the valley, we knew many of the workers and activists in the area.

The workers arrived at the Wenger Desert Chapel in small groups. Although it was late in fall, the desert sun was still intense, hanging brightly over the rocky desert hills. Some of the men bore the farm workers' flag, the black eagle emblazoned on a background of red and white. Maria Esquivel, another of the strikers, brought a banner of the *Virgen de Guadalupe*.

Before the services began, the chapel was filled to capacity. Only a handful of Anglos were in attendance. The mourners were mostly Mexican-American farm workers, students, and welfare recipients. Alfredo Figueroa and his brother Miguel were there. Alfredo brought his guitar, which he claimed made life bearable while he was in jail.

Caswell's relatives had disowned him and refused to cover the expenses of the funeral. The poor people of the valley took up a collection and Ed Gorges, a former employer and close friend of Caswell, made a generous contribution for the casket.

A Protestant minister arrived and conferred with Jim Drake and myself. He had learned of our participation in the service and warned us against making a "political rally" out of the funeral. The funeral director asked us not to sing or make our contributions too lengthy, since they were running under a "tight schedule."

The funeral directors and the professional religionist provided a sharp contrast to the humble grandeur of the workers. Perhaps it was fitting that the former were present at Jim's funeral. They were so symbolic of the society that Jim Caswell had challenged and tried to change.

Jim Drake read from the Scriptures and concluded his reading with a brief commentary. The power structure had taken away Jim Caswell's rights. He died a poor man and an outcast. But nobody could take away the power of his presence in the valley of Coachella. Nobody could stamp out the memory of a man who had changed the lives of so many of its poor. Drake concluded with an expression the workers often use in showing affection for their friends: *Que viva Jim Caswell!* (Long live Jim Caswell!)

We sang on the way to the cemetery, walking three abreast behind the funeral coach. Alfredo Figueroa strummed three songs from the strike on his guitar: *Solidaridad para Siempre (Solidarity Forever), De Colores,* and *Nosotros Venceremos.* Men, women, and children openly wept as we arrived at the burial site.

After a few prayers had been said, Amalia Uribe, a pretty, dark-skinned College of the Desert sophomore, spoke passionately, telling the bystanders how Jim Caswell had helped her and several other students, a few of whom were also in attendance. Her voice faded into sobs.

Alfredo Figueroa spoke next, his voice choked with emotion. "I was with Jim in prison," he said. "They wouldn't give him his medicine. He was like a baby deprived of his mother's milk. He was like grass that has no water and dries up. . . . Long live the memory of this great man, Jim Caswell!" Two friends supported Figueroa, his face frozen in solemn grief.

The closing prayer was fitting for Caswell's interment.

We pray that nothing of this man's life be lost, but that it will be of benefit to the world; that all that he held sacred may be respected by those who follow him and that everything in which he was great may continue to mean much now that he is dead. We ask you that he may go on living in our hearts and minds, in our courage and conscience. Amen.

After the obsequies, the mourners walked slowly back to the funeral chapel. The Chocolate Mountains shimmered under the heat of the midday sun. The abandoned shacks and labor camps of the harvest hands looked desolate as we passed them on our way to Indio. The vineyards awaited pruning and the beginning of another yearly cycle of birth, fruition, and death.

One of the Mexican-American women, who wore a black lace mantilla, folded a memorial card and placed it between the pages of a tattered prayerbook. On the card were inscribed the words:

In Memory of:
James Samuel Caswell, Born June 14, 1920, Canada
Passed Away, November 19, 1969, Riverside
Services: November 24, 1969
Wenger Desert Chapel, Indio, California

In April, 1970, Jim Caswell and his fellow convicts received their reprieve. In a 6 to 1 decision, the court set aside the convictions of Caswell, Figueroa, Kay, and Loya. The court stated:

The sentence was far more severe than any we have been able to discover in other prosecutions for disturbing a meeting. . . . The clap-in demonstration represented an acceptable nonviolent expression of alternative viewpoints. . . . The petitioners' protest was protected by the First Amendment right of free speech.

Justice came too late for Jim Caswell, but the poor of the Coachella Valley are not likely to forget about him for a long time to come.

[10]

Cesar Chavez
on Nonviolence

Nonviolence is a phenomenon that has been closely examined by students and scholars. Sociologists who feel they have seismographic insights regarding the political mood of the country tell us that nonviolence is making a quiet return across the nation. But one wonders if nonviolence was present in the United States in the first place. Thomas Merton once said that our ability to destroy life and pollute our environment is a by-product of a widespread sense of insecurity. A recent John Wayne movie captures the frontier spirit of the old West. Wayne guns a man down and piously states that the Lord would have wanted it that way.

Radical students and militants of every stamp have pooh-poohed nonviolence in recent years. Cesar has said that these people either do not understand it or have been unsuccessful in implementing it in their lives.

Chavez's concept of nonviolence is bound up with his own deep religious convictions as well as with his superb

ability as a tactician. Cesar Chavez is both a mystic vision-
ary and a pragmatist, with a heavy accent on the latter. As
a student of social movements and forces, he knows that
violence can only breed more violence. It leads to a tragic
escalation that ends in the demoralization of one's forces.
As a Christian, Chavez has a deep reverence for human life.

I recently told Cesar about some good news I had received. After ten years of praying and waiting for a baby
to come along, my sister's prayers had been answered. Her
plans of adopting a second child were altered by the fact
that she was to have one of her own. Cesar smiled and said,
"Viva vida." "Long live life." The thought struck me so
strongly that I preached on the subject of human life the
following Sunday at Guadalupe Church. As I scanned the
congregation at the nine o'clock Mass, I noticed Cesar sitting in the middle of the church, flanked by his two bodyguards, Macario Bustos and Ray Olivos. I wondered what
he thought about the sermon, since it was really inspired
by some of our conversations about human life and human
dignity.

Nonviolence is a strong motivating force that expresses
itself in a million ways. When one rejects the destructive
forces of violence, one must be creative in order to
survive. Cesar has invented so many ways to express nonviolent struggle that his opposition has labeled him "theat-
rical" and his organization a circus. But, whether the farm
workers were having a Mass, a picket line, a religious procession, a fast, a sit-in, or any kind of demonstration, Cesar
has been able to preserve the spirit of nonviolent struggle
among his people. The important element, according to
Chavez, is not just to win the struggle, but how you win it.
If respect for life or truth has been lost, then something
essential is missing.

In recent years, Delano, California, has been the mecca
for those who seek social change through nonviolent means.
One of its most recent foreign visitors was a young law

student from Mexico City. Pablo Monroy, a handsome, smiling, dark-complexioned Mexican arrived in Delano, equipped with a tape-recorder, a camera, and a mission from his fellow-students. He was to learn about nonviolence from one of the few men who has made it work.

Cesar Chavez was tired when Pablo and I arrived at his modest home on Kensington Street. He had just finished a tough negotiating session with two Delano grape growers. His wife, Helen, was busy preparing a meal for him, and Pablo and I were invited to join the meal.

Cesar asked Pablo how things were with the student movement in Mexico City since the bitter repression just before the Olympic games. Hundreds had died in a government-sponsored bloodbath when soldiers fired on a student rally. Pablo responded that there was little activity, that everything had gone underground. He and a group of students were arrested and imprisoned when they conducted a fast protesting the government policies. They held their fast in front of the cathedral in the *zocalo,* or city square.

As Pablo spoke, he familiarized himself with the surroundings in the Chavez home. Above a bookcase were the high school graduation pictures of two of the Chavez daughters, Sylvia and Linda. On an opposite wall hung a portrait of Our Lady of Guadalupe, and nearby was a statue of Martin de Porres, the patron saint of Mexico's poor and oppressed. Through the open door of a bedroom, we could see Cesar's two youngest sons, Anthony and Paul, doing their homework, sprawled on a double bed. Anthony, nicknamed Birdie, was fending off a puppy, who was biting on his pant leg. In one corner of the living room, a large German shepherd named Boycott sat, sniffing at the aroma from the kitchen. Boycott is Cesar's watchdog.

"Nonviolence is not cowardice," Cesar began. "A nonviolent person cannot be fearful. He must be on his toes at all times. He must be a strategist. He must know how to deal with people, above all. You see, nonviolence means that you involve people in creative ways. The real force of nonviolence is in numbers."

Pablo riveted his eyes on Chavez, noting his every gesture. Cesar speaks with his hands and conveys his feelings with every expression of his face. Pablo began to ask questions about organizing.

"Your meetings have to be short and to the point," Cesar continued. "There is nothing more disastrous than to have meetings which ramble on and on without any results. In order to organize successfully, you must have some clearly defined goals. And, when you organize, you must do it bit by bit, very deliberately and carefully. It's like digging a ditch. You take one shovelful at a time. And, in order to have some progress, you need examples of success. Each minor victory builds up a spirit among the people.

"No leader is violent by nature," Chavez said, in a low voice. "Very often violence is used by an individual in order to overthrow another leader. It is used like a tool. It is in vogue now. But, deep down in their hearts, these people do not really believe in violence."

Pablo told how difficult it was to keep the movement going in Mexico City while one is tied to class attendance or to holding down a job. "In order to build a successful nonviolent movement, you must be involved in it night and day," Cesar replied. "You must be occupied with it constantly. You must do nothing more and nothing less than the movement. Nonviolence depends on the absolute loyalty of the leadership to their cause, and the ability of the leadership to attract and organize other people."

Helen served us supper. Cesar was served a vegetarian plate. Pablo hardly noticed the food placed before him as he continued to listen attentively to Cesar's ideas, which he wove into a narrative of the five-year-long grape struggle.

Cesar began to recount the early days of the strike. "When the strike began," he said, "there were over 100 arrests. Twenty-five of our pickets were severely beaten by

growers and policemen. Extra sheriff's deputies were assigned to Delano. When the growers beat us, we did not
fight back. Finally, they began to respect us for this."

Helen finished her work in the kitchen and sat down
beside us as Cesar spoke about the spirit of sacrifice inherent in the Mexican and Filipino farm workers who walked
out of the vineyards on strike in 1965. "Our people are
ready to accept sacrifices. They have made many sacrifices
in the decades of exploitation and humiliation they have
faced as agricultural workers. They are ready to undergo
more sacrifices in the course of their liberation. A year after
the strike began, our people were willing to march 300
miles to Sacramento in order to witness to the validity and
justice of their cause. In addition to this, the strikers have
been willing to live without wages. The union only takes
care of their basic needs, such as rent, clothing, and food.
Once people are willing to make these sacrifices, you develop a power of the spirit which can affect your adver-
saries in ways you can hardly imagine. Gandhi called this
power 'moral jujitsu.'

"I am firmly convinced that nonviolence cannot exist
only in books or on the seminar level on our university
campuses, but it must exist in the flesh. I have always
believed that people are the most important element we
have. We must put flesh into our nonviolence rather than
simply talk about it."

As he speaks, Chavez presents a picture of raw determination. He has often said that, in the twenty years he has
spent as an organizer in the barrios and rural areas of
California, the most important lesson he has learned is
the discipline required to organize effectively. "Until you
achieve the goal you set out to accomplish, never let an
adversary rest or a bad situation get worse," Cesar has
said. Chavez likes the Spanish phrase *encaprichado a ven-
cer:* deadset, or hell-bent, on victory. During his twenty-
five day fast for nonviolence, many people tried to force
him to eat or at least drink some soup or juice, but he

refused. "You know how he is," his cousin Manuel Chavez would remark, *"encaprichado como un Indio."* "Stubborn like an Indian."

"When you take on an adversary you must have some good, solid, tough issues—the tougher the better. If you have a good cause, you can have success. You can't have something undefinable to fight for; you need a solid wall of opposition in order to make an impact." Cesar clenched his right fist and made contact with the palm of his left hand, which he held vertically. "If your opposition is unclear and undefined, it's like making an impact with a bowl of mush. This is what happens most of the time people get together to fight the welfare or the police or any agency which is oppressing them. They get into a fight, but nothing happens. Pretty soon they ask each other: What is happening? What are we doing? Are we getting anywhere?

"The other thing you have to remember," Chavez continued, "is that you must carry on your campaign morally, legally, and nonviolently."

Cesar paused for a moment, then recalled the critical phases of the campaign against Di Giorgio Farms. "They were out to destroy our union," Cesar related. "Our pickets were being beaten and harassed by the foremen and the police. The spirit among the strikers was very low, almost to the level of complete hopelessness. Then, some women came to the office from the small farm workers' town of Earlimart, ten miles north of Delano. They were on strike with us, so I thought they had come to bring me another problem. One of them had a suggestion. 'Pardon us, Mr. Chavez, but we think we have a way to make some progress with the strike. Why don't we start a prayer novena at the entrance to the Di Giorgio property? We could bring a statue of the Virgen de Guadalupe, and some candles. We could make a small altar.' The whole thing just about knocked me off my chair. It was a perfect idea, and one I never would have thought of! I immediately got on the phone and called a few priest friends in different parts of California. We set up the altar on the back of an old station wagon. Several of our people began an around-the-clock prayer vigil. We got on the radio and announced that there would be a Mass each day during the novena. People started to come to the Masses from all over. The pressure on Di Giorgio was fantastic. There were great crowds of farm workers and supporters praying and singing at the entrance to the Di Giorgio vineyards. The one thing that bound the strikers and the Di Giorgio workers together was their common Catholic faith. One of the workers later told me of a moving scene inside one of the vineyards. One of the workers who had just voted in favor of representation by the union held up a picture of Our Lady of Guadalupe and, with tears in his eyes, cried, 'May she protect us!' It was during this time that Di Giorgio foremen were sending around goon squads to beat up on union sympathizers.

"At these prayer meetings, the workers got a chance to know the strikers. The foreman has spread vicious rumors about us, and this served to break down a lot of the suspicion and fears. I would say that the vigils we had were a decisive factor in winning the Di Giorgio campaign. The beautiful thing about it was this: The ideas came from the workers themselves. When you search out these ideas from among the people you can get out of almost any jam. This is the real meaning of nonviolence, as far as I'm concerned. The leadership of any movement must be awake to these ideas. Let me tell you, all the experts predicted that we would lose the Di Giorgio elections; the labor writers and all the TV people openly stated that we would lose. They even took bets against us in Las Vegas. But the strikers were creative. They worked hard, and we won."

I looked at my watch. It was already 9:00 P.M. I had promised Cesar that we would not take up too much of his time. Luckily, there were no callers, which is unusual in Cesar's home. He has mentioned that the union never

sleeps. Long after the UFWOC office staff returns home
from work, problems continually crop up and usually land
at the Chavez home.

A puppy ran under the supper table as Cesar finished
the last few morsels on his plate. Cesar picked up the animal, stroked it, and handed it to his daughter Ana.

"It all boils down to a lot of tedious organizing and a
lot of hard work. It has been rough on the family, but they
have been great. My first organizing in the valley entailed
a lot of driving—getting home sometimes at two and three
in the morning. I covered every small town in the San
Joaquin Valley from the Tehachapi Mountains in the
south to Marysville in the north, some 450 miles. Initially,
I made contact with about eighty-six families. The workers
themselves chipped in and kept our family stocked with
meat and fresh vegetables. I would help the workers with
whatever problems they had—problems with the welfare
department, the police department, disability cases, etc.
We call this service work, much similar to what a social
worker does. By 1962, we had about 211 members and
held our first convention, calling ourselves the National
Farm Workers Association.

"My brother Richard, who is a carpenter by trade, called
my organizing 'ridiculous.' 'How are you ever going to
take on these big growers here in Delano?' he would ask
me. He never believed it could be done. But we did.''

[11]

A Farm Worker Becomes Bishop

The episcopal ordination of Patrick Fernandez Flores in San Antonio, Texas, was a beautiful event. It was a sign of hope when set in the context of the historic struggle of the Chicanos for recognition in the Southwest. It is no secret that the Catholic Church in the Southwest has lagged behind in the fight for social justice among the Spanish-speaking. In very few instances does the Church speak relevantly to these people.

In many areas, church leaders have not only alienated forward-thinking Chicanos but have also embittered them and made them anticlerical. Los Angeles is a case in point. The church could have worked effectively with a new organization of young Chicanos called *Catolicos por la Raza* (Catholics for the Mexican Race). Instead, the hierarchy sanctioned a violent police reaction against one of the picket lines protesting in front of St. Basil's Church, a new $3 million edifice on Wilshire Boulevard. The young

Chicanos were protesting the expense of the building and the apathetic response of the Catholic Church to the social problems in East Los Angeles, an explosive and poverty-stricken Mexican-American ghetto.

The ministry and leadership of the church is generally fearful when faced with such questions as the economic exploitation of the Chicano, police brutality, substandard housing and medical care, demoralizing poverty programs, hostile welfare services, and racist and dead-end educational institutions.

There is no other institution that needs the pressure of the power of poor people more than the church. There is no institution that has more of a potential for creating social change than the church. Therefore, when a former migratory farm worker who has lived in shacks and suffered the lot of the downtrodden dons an episcopal mitre, one's heart is warmed. And, when Patrick Flores tells his fellow Chicanos not to be afraid to criticize the church but to change it if necessary, one experiences a profound sense of hope.

The more skeptical believe that the Flores consecration represents a kind of tokenism. But those who believe in the power of the poor know that tokenism is an evil you allow to happen. If the Chicanos want more bishops to represent them, they will get them—in El Paso, Tucson, Los Angeles, Fresno, Denver, Yakima, and wherever they are oppressed and need someone in high places to help them achieve justice. These men will not miraculously appear on the scene, however. Someone is going to have to fight for them.

Cesar and I talked about the significance of the Flores event as we traveled back to Delano by plane. Senator Ralph Yarborough had just been defeated by a right-wing oilman in the Texas Democratic primary, and Chicano politicians in Texas seemed more intent on cutting each other's throats than on advancing the cause of *la raza*. Yarborough was under fire for not effectively organizing his campaign and going after the Chicano vote. Cesar spoke to this point with a look of disgust on his face. "You can't expect to get anywhere unless you build an organization and work like hell to reach your goal. Why can't these guys see that they have to spend their time organizing?" he said, pounding the armrest with the palm of his hand. Cesar was tired. As the plane crossed the barren wasteland of west Texas, he made a remark about the vast job of organizing the farm workers in the Southwest. His mind returned to the Flores event, and he smiled and said that the Mass had been beautiful. When I looked at him again, he was asleep.

In his youth, Patrick Fernandez Flores picked cotton as a migratory farm worker in Texas. He lived with his parents and his eight brothers and sisters in sheds and barns on the outskirts of the farm towns between Corpus Christi and Amarillo. When Apostolic Delegate Archbishop Luigi Raimondi pronounced the words of episcopal consecration to Father Flores on May 5, applause and cries of *Viva la Raza!* rose from the ranks of the faithful. The event took place at the Convention Center Arena in San Antonio before a crowd of 8,000 worshipers.

The consecration ceremony was colorful and people-oriented, with a minimum of occult ritual and pomp. Chicano militants were amused, however, at the foppish, militaristic appearance of the Knights of Columbus members who led the opening procession to the altar. One of the young Brown Berets, who sported a Chicano-power button on his army fatigue jacket, gazed at the sword-bearing and feather-hatted warriors of God's people and asked me, "Who are those heavy dudes, man?" He added that the mitred bishops (fifteen strong) reminded him of the Ku Klux Klan.

Two Mexican *mariachi* bands intoned the *Misa Panamericana* as the Mass began. Colorful banners were placed on the altar—one of them bore Flores's motto in

Spanish: *Trabajaré, no por mi mismo, sino para vosotros*
(I will not work for myself, but for all of you). Another
read: "A man for all seasons."

Outside the arena, there had been a minor protest—
leaflets were passed out denouncing the presence of Cesar
Chavez, José Angel Gutierrez, a militant Chicano leader
and head of the new Raza Unida Party in Texas's Rio
Grande Valley, and Bishop Sergio Mendez Arceo of Cuernavaca, Mexico. (Mendez arrived a day later for a related
celebration in Houston.)

Among several church dignitaries seated at the altar was
the slight figure of Cesar Chavez who had been invited to
read from the Second Epistle of Saint Paul to the Corinth-
ians. "One man died for all so that all men would not live
for themselves, but for others," he read.

I could not avoid asking myself the question that must
have been in the minds of so many people in the arena that
day. Were these words and these symbols speaking the
truth to the Chicanos in Texas? Can the institutional
church still speak with Paul of reconciliation and the New
Creation to people it has ignored for so long? Does the
consecration of Bishop Flores represent a new policy of
the hierarchy for minority peoples, or does it represent a
cruel form of tokenism? Will Flores be the first of many
Mexican-American bishops desperately needed in the
Southwest?

José Angel Gutierrez, a thin, mustachioed young man in
his late twenties applauded during the ceremony, but these
nagging doubts and questions were on his mind, too.

"The church has failed us miserably," Gutierrez told me.
"The ax has fallen on several priests in Texas who have
become actively involved on behalf of the Chicanos. Archbishop Furey, of San Antonio, is beginning to help us by
establishing an Archdiocesan Council on Mexican-American Affairs. But we have found the clergy totally detached
from the needs of the poor. In Rio Grande City, a $1 mil-
lion church was built just after the farm workers went on

strike for mere survival wages. The new church building is really obscene in light of the miserable conditions in which the Chicanos live. Priests drive late-model cars and live in three- and four-bedroom air-conditioned houses, while the average wage of a farm worker in Zavala County is $1,754, and only $1,534 in La Salle County. It's bad enough to face repression from the police and the political machine, but, when you get it from the church, as we have, it's really hard to take. We now have some sympathetic bishops, but the clergy by and large have abandoned us."

Patrick Flores has proven himself a warm and lovable pastor as well as a capable administrator in the parishes he served in Houston and nearby Pasadena, Texas. His pastoral concerns have been directed toward the Christian Family Movement, the Cursillo Movement, and the Catholic Youth Organization. The younger clergy have found him to be an able counselor. His personal friendship with Cesar Chavez and his affection for Chicano militants have prevented anyone from hanging the *Tio Taco* (Uncle Tom) label on him.

In an interview with the Alamo, Texas, *Messenger*, Flores stated that the gap between those who speak for justice and those who struggle for it must be closed. He pledged his efforts to gain better wages, housing, job opportunities, and other advantages for the poor, especially Chicanos. Mexican-Americans comprise 43 per cent of the nearly 800,000 residents of San Antonio.

During an evening Mass celebrated at San Antonio's Mission San José, the new Bishop listened to an impassioned speech by José Angel Gutierrez, who said that "our church needs criticism, and it needs to be returned to the people. If we don't criticize it, we will lose it, as the church has been lost for so many years." Gutierrez added that he would like to remember Flores as the first Mexican-American bishop and not the only one. Earlier in the day, Cesar Chavez had told a reporter from the *San Antonio Express* that the consecration of Bishop Flores was a "miracle" and a "recognition of the Mexican-American Catholic." He spoke of his warm friendship with Flores and voiced the hope that the Bishop's elevation "will be the first of several for Mexican Americans in the Southwest."

A lasting remembrance of Bishop Patrick Flores was my brief encounter with him as he left his hotel in San Antonio en route to the episcopal ordination. He was singing a lively Mexican song with a group of nuns. He approached me, gave me a warm *abrazo*, the traditional Mexican embrace, and said, smiling, "I'm Father Flores. I'm happy to know you. Thanks for coming."

With that, he began to lead the nuns in the song *De Colores*, picked up a tiny girl, and, carrying her in his arms, boarded the Greyhound bus that took him to the convention center and his episcopal ordination.

[12]

Delano: A View from the West Side

Our Lady of Guadalupe Church is located on the corner of Eleventh and Clinton streets, on the west side of Delano. The west side is populated mostly by Mexican-American, Filipino and black farm workers. During the grape strike, a small percentage of these workers stayed on as full-time strikers and worked at the union's headquarters at Forty Acres.

Although some of the workers, including Cesar Chavez and his family, live on the east side, Delano is separated physically as well as racially by the Southern Pacific Railroad tracks. The town's Anglo population lives on the east side, with the Mexican-Americans, Filipinos, and blacks on the west side.

Guadalupe Church was heavily financed by the grape growers when it was built some fifteen years ago. As a gesture of their paternalism, the farmers left their names impressed on the church pews and on the stained-glass windows. I was made aware of this when an irate grower telephoned me in the summer of 1968. He warned me against marching and demonstrating with Chavez and his union. He reminded me that his family had donated stained-glass windows to the church. When he became a bit nasty and threatening during the phone conversation, I told him to come and take the windows back. "You aren't going to buy *me* off, buddy," I told him. I have since regretted making the remark. He had no idea what I was talking about; as tough as he was, I tend to think I hurt his feelings.

Cesar Chavez took his strike vote in the parish hall at Guadalupe Church in September, 1965. The grape growers never forgave the pastor, Father Francis X. Alabart, for allowing Chavez and his followers the use of the hall. They harassed him by making insulting phone calls at night, telling him that he had betrayed their interests.

Alabart has been criticized by both sides for his allegedly fearful and vacillating stand on the grape strike. The truth of the matter is that the man had been deeply wounded by the harsh treatment he received from the growers. He often stated that the workers had never insulted or offended him in that fashion.

The same grower control exists in every town in the valley. To the extent that the workers build a powerful union, this arrogance of the employers and townsfolk will disappear.

The following chapter contains a few reflections of life on the west side. It was written during the spring and early summer of 1970, when the Delano growers arrived at their decision to sit down and talk with Cesar Chavez and his union.

The organization of farm workers will undoubtedly bring about many improvements in Delano and many other rural communities like it throughout the United

States. An account of some recent events that took place in Delano will give the reader an idea of what kind of changes are necessary.

Roberto Garcia was found dead, apparently of a heart attack, in his humble shack on Delano's west side. His daughter, Ana, a married woman of about thirty-five years of age, arrived the next day from Los Angeles to identify the body and make the funeral arrangements.

Ana had been bitter against the Catholic Church for many years. She explained to me that her mother had died when she was a small child and that she had been raised by nuns in an orphanage. The sisters, she claims, warped her outlook on life on everything from sex to her identity as a Mexican American.

Ana feels free to talk to me because I simply listen to her without pronouncing any sanctimonious judgments or saccharine moralisms. I tended to agree with many of the things she told me, but it is difficult for me to see how the church could be quite so bad as she claims it is—that is, it could not be responsible for *all* the evil in the world.

I accompanied Ana to the funeral parlor to make the necessary arrangements. She explained that she did not want any Mass or rosary, because, although her father was baptized a Catholic, he never really accepted, in her words, "all the baloney that goes under the name of Christianity."

"He was an Indian from Mexico," she told me. "He always thought that priests were a bunch of *huevones* [lazy drones] and used to teach me Indian poems and prayers. Christianity should have stayed in Europe, where it could have done more good. The Indians led rather peaceful lives before the conquering Christians arrived."

I got a call later on that evening that the rest of the family insisted on having a rosary and a Mass. There were about thirty people in the church the next morning. The scene resembled a Bergman movie. I have always found it agonizing to officiate at a funeral when the people present are completely alienated from the symbols and rituals of the Mass and funeral services. This was certainly the case with the Garcia funeral. But the worst was yet to come.

When I got to the cemetery, one of the caretakers pointed to a plot that had not yet been prepared. "I told them at the funeral parlor that the grave wouldn't be ready this morning," he drawled. I looked with amazement at the man. "You mean it's not even dug yet?" I asked. "That's right," he told me, shrugging his shoulders.

The family was shocked and embarrassed when they saw what had happened. We had to return three hours later to complete the burial services. As it turned out, the mortician blamed the cemetery director, and vice versa. There had been a long-standing feud between the two, and Roberto Garcia, a Mexican farm worker, was its victim.

I wrote a letter to the mayor of Delano and sent copies to the city councilmen. I also contacted one of the county Board of Supervisors members by phone. In my letter to Clifford Loader, mayor of Delano, I explained what had happened and concluded the letter as follows: "Roberto Garcia was a farm worker. I am certain this would never happen to the so-called better families of Delano, Mr. Mayor, and I think you know what I mean. If you would like me to elaborate on this, I am free to do so at any time you wish."

The funeral-parlor director later called me and asked me for a copy of the letter I had sent to the city council. It just so happened that the mayor and city council officials had "lost" the copies that I had sent them. He had scheduled a hearing with the board of directors of the cemetery district and wanted to add my testimony to a long list of grievances he had with the caretaker. I never found out who was directly to blame. The fact that it might never happen again was little consolation to the family of Roberto Garcia.

Two days later, Esteban Lopez arrived in his battered Ford at the office of our newspaper, *El Malcriado,* at Forty

Farm workers' picket line in Salinas, California *Photo: Cris Sanchez*

The home of the UFWOC newspaper *El Malcriado,* at Forty Acres   *Photo: Bob Thurber*

A farm worker's house, in Earlimart, California

At right, James Caswell (left) and Bert Corona, in Indio, California

Below, Cesar Chavez breaking his twenty-five–day fast, on March 10, 1968, and sharing bread with the late Senator Robert Kennedy *Photo: Gene Daniels*

Gil Padilla (left) and Antonio Orendain (right)
— two of UFWOC's most important leaders

Mayor John Lindsay greeting, in 1969, New York boycott leaders Maria Saludado (center), a Mexican American, and Andy and Luming Imutan, originally members of the largely Filipino Agricultural Workers Organizing Committee, which started the Delano grape strike *Photo: Stanley Randal*

Al Rojas, UFWOC organizer, at a 1969 boycott rally in Pittsburgh, Pennsylvania

Patrick Coyne, United Steelworkers of America, and Father Jack O'Malley, both arrested for supporting the 1969 Pittsburgh grape boycott

Workers marching from Coachella to Calexico, in May, 1969

Photo: George Ballis

UFWOC organizer Pete Velasco (left) and Dr. Ralph Abernathy (center), during the 1969 march to the border town of Calexico before the Coachella grape strike *Photo: Steve Kahn*

Desire Rojas, after Labor Day, 1968, demonstration in Los Angeles

Salinas farm workers receiving their strike benefits after a week of picketing *Photo: Bob Fitch*

At left, September, 1970, strike at a cabbage field in Salinas, California *Photo: Cris Sanchez*

Guards, hired by the growers, patrolling the fields during the strike *Photos: Bob Fitch*

Salinas Valley farm workers attending a memorial Mass, in September, 1970, for thirty-one Mexican *braceros* who were killed when their truck collided with a train near Chualar, California *Photo: Cris Sanchez*

Chavez and, at the right, the Reverends Chris Hartmire and Victor Salandini after their arrest in the summer of 1966

Bishop Hugh Donohoe (standing) at May, 1970, press conference announcing contracts between UFWOC and Delano growers Bruno Dispoto (far left) and Anthony Bianco (far right) *Photo: Central California Register*

Grower John Giumarra, with hands raised, after he signed contract with UFWOC *Photo: Cris Sanchez*

Acres. He patiently waited as I finished a telephone call
and then asked if I or someone in the union could help
him with a problem he and his wife had at the Delano
Hospital. I would not have believed his story if I had
heard it secondhand. But, as Esteban spoke, slowly and
very calmly, I knew that he was not exaggerating in the
least. He showed me a copy of a letter that a neighbor had
helped him compose. The letter was addressed to Mayor
Loader.

Honorable Mayor,
   I realize that the following problem my wife and I had
is really not the problem of the city; however, I feel I must
state my feelings so that what has happened to me and my
wife does not happen again.
   On December 20, 1969, at 6 P.M., I took my wife, Maria
Lopez, to the Delano Hospital. She was in pain, and delivery
was expected at any moment. She was admitted and put in
room 112. I was in constant contact with her and tried to
get the attention of the nurses, who were amused at my not
being able to make myself understood.
   They only paid attention to my wife after she had
screamed several times, and the initial yell of my new born
son was heard.
   There was no doctor in attendance nor nurses. When they
did arrive they had to clean the child, who was suffocating
from his own fluids.
   Not even an animal is left by himself to bear his offspring.
If we cannot trust our own local hospital and doctors, who
do we go to? I want to know to whom I can speak about
this outrage! The hospital even had the nerve to charge me
for the delivery room: $70.00.
   I am bringing this to your attention for the simple reason
that I do not want it to happen again.

Sincerely yours,
ESTEBAN LOPEZ

When I finished reading the letter, Lopez handed me
the reply he had received from the mayor:

Dear Mr. Lopez,

Thank you for your letter of December 23rd, telling me
about the problem that you had at the Delano Hospital.

You are right that it is not a problem of the city government. However, I shall refer your letter to the doctor.

I appreciate your writing to me and I hope you will not
have any problems in the future.

> Sincerely,
> CLIFFORD L. LOADER

The case was taken up by some rural legal-assistance
attorney, but never advanced beyond the initial stages.

Two weeks later, Mexican-American students walked
out of Delano High School because of the school's attitude toward minority-group students. In sworn affidavits, students told how teachers called Mexican students
"beaners." Several of the students were told to go back to
Mexico if they disliked the school's policies or its teachers.
Most of the students were sons and daughters of farm
laborers. At the height of the walkout, a hundred students
were picketing the high school. Several of them were suspended for their activities. Two of the seniors who walked
out and were refused their diplomas were Eloise Chavez,
Cesar's daughter, and Dorothy Chavez, his niece.

Two weeks later, on the evening of the Delano High
School graduation ceremonies, all hell broke loose. I was
on my way to the Delano bus station to pick up Brother
Jerry, a Franciscan brother who had just arrived from
Sacramento, when two girls shouted to me from the street
and said that there had been a riot at the high school and
that several people were arrested. When I arrived at the
police station, a crowd was gathering. Most of them were
Mexican-American farm workers and their sons and daughters. A few blacks mingled with the crowd. Everyone was
angry. Father Al, the pastor of Guadalupe Church, was
talking to John Ortega and Jerome McManigal, two attorneys from the California Rural Legal Assistance. The

police would not allow the attorneys to attend the booking procedure. The local judge had mysteriously disappeared. This meant that the students who were arrested could not be released on bail until the following Monday.

The crowd began to press around the outside of the jail. Five plainclothes officers moved through the crowd and stationed themselves at the doorway. "That's the one! That's the cop who beat up on my brother in the police car," shouted one of the students. The policeman shot a hostile glance at the boy and rubbed his leather-fisted hands together. "You see them gloves, man," a black youth pointed at the officer. "They wear them for the dirty work. They use them when they beat us up, so their hands will stay nice and clean." The gloves looked like handball mittens, with a thick-black-suede texture. The police began to talk with one another, joking about the brown berets the students wore. They laughed, but they were nervous and uneasy. The crowd was getting larger and more hostile.

I heard some painful cries emanating from the jail. The crowd began to move in that direction, in back of the police station. The cries were from Freddie, Cesar's college-age nephew. He had been arrested with the rest of the students when he protested the treatment of Connie Rangel. Captain Harry Gilbert of the Delano Police Department was standing near the entrance to the jail, and I approached him. "What do you want?" he asked.

"Freddie just had an operation on his arm and he's in pain," I said. "Why don't you release him and have a doctor look at it?"

"We can't do anything until the booking procedure is finished," he said.

Freddie screamed again and again. I yelled back to him, "Take it easy, Freddie, we'll get you a doctor!" Marion Moses, the union's nurse, arrived a short time later, and was able to have Freddie released for a medical examination. Shortly thereafter, I drove Connie Rangel to the Delano Hospital to have her examined. She appeared to be in a state of minor shock after her encounter with the police.

When I arrived back at the police station, I was met by some fifty policemen and sheriff's deputies, all in riot gear. I asked Captain Gilbert what was happening. "I might ask you that question, Father," he said sarcastically. "You seem to be the head agitator around here." At that point, I assured him that if there was to be any riot that night, it would probably be instigated by the police. The reason for the entire brigade was a rumor started by the police. A busload of youngsters was returning late that night to west Delano from a visit to Disneyland. The police thought that the adults who were waiting for their children to return home were discontented farm workers about to start a riot. Hence the massive deployment of troops and the riot gear.

While I stood in front of the jail, I talked to some of the students who had been at the earlier high school graduation. The high school administration, bracing for trouble, had stationed plainclothes men at the entrance to the graduation ceremonies. Most of the striking students had tickets to the ceremonies. When Connie Rangel approached the ticket gate, the high school principal spotted her and told the police not to admit her, even though she had a ticket. She protested and was pushed to the ground by a policeman. Connie was at that time eight months pregnant. Her father and mother came to her assistance. But they were set upon by more police.

In the melee that ensued, Connie's father, Julian, and her brother Mike were the first to be arrested. In the next few minutes, Mr. and Mrs. Faustino Cervantes were arrested. A short while later, the total arrested grew to fifteen, three adults and twelve teenagers.

Because I missed the incidents at the high school, I asked one of the young girls what had transpired. "All of a sudden, the cops grabbed Mike Rangel," she said. "He yelled at them for pushing his sister around. Three cops started to beat up on him. They were kind of choking him. And then I started crying because I told them not to do anything to him. Then the cops started grabbing the other kids who were just looking on. When they told them to go to the police car, they just went on ahead, but the cops were the ones that started everything. I remember that my sister went up to one of the policemen who was choking a boy. She said, 'Don't ever hold him like that. He's not a dog.' They tried to arrest her, but she got back to the ticket line."

Another girl, Rosie Serrano, observed the arrest of Mrs. Cervantes. "They pushed her into the car, and she was kicking, and they were hitting her. They were putting some gas [Mace] in her mouth and on her face. They couldn't stick her in the car, so they got a paddy wagon and stuck her in there."

The officer who arrested Mrs. Cervantes later filed a report of the incident. His report to the chief of police read:

> Due to the great difficulty I and several other officers were having with her I felt that maybe the mace would subdue her. I wanted to subdue her quickly as there was a very large crowd of angry people there. The mace only made her fight harder. She was then removed to a paddy wagon and transported to the police station. I would like to add that I have had the occasion to use the mace three times on combative people. Each time they only became more combative after its application. The gas nearly always gets into the eyes of the officer plus other officers, and the transporting officer and booking officer also suffer from its use. Respectfully submitted. Billy H. Mayo. Sergeant, Watch One.

On the following day, the adults were released. The juveniles were not released until Monday. About a week later, Joe Huerta, one of the boys who had been arrested, was sent to the Delano hospital for observation. A medical report showed that he had a malignant testicle. A police officer had kicked him in the groin. Joe told me that he was standing near a police car and an officer told him to get in. When he asked why, the officer gave him a knee in the groin, which doubled him over in pain. He was then thrown into the police car.

The newspapers carried the police report issued by Captain Gilbert. Gilbert said that a mob of 200 persons, led by UFWOC's Larry Itliong (assistant director of the union), stormed the Delano jail and slashed tires on "several police cars."

The full text of Gilbert's report was incredible to anyone who was present either at the high school or at the police station. Gilbert maintained that the students and their parents had attacked the police and attempted to take the prisoners from the jail. He also claimed that Father Dave Duran, myself, and Marion Moses had tried to force our way through the rear of the police station. "Marion Moses and the priest shouted obscenities at me and the other officers, stating that we were all a bunch of f——— pigs, bastards, etc., demanding that Freddie Chavez be released immediately or they would take him by force."

The next day, the people involved in the episode met at UFWOC headquarters at Forty Acres, but very little was resolved. Mrs. Cervantes could hardly walk. Her body was covered with bruises—the result of the beating administered by the arresting officers.

Meanwhile, the police kept close surveillance on the striking Chicano students all summer, and the kids were a constant target of abuse and innuendo by the *Delano Record*.

John Ortega, a young Chicano attorney from the McFarland office of the California Rural Legal Assistance, had been handling the case of the youths from the beginning of the school strike. He was eventually dropped from the case by his superiors at CRLA for his allegedly imprudent actions while counseling the students. His supporters maintained that, when the attorneys stuck their necks out to defend someone, their actions were considered "political" and "dangerous." Several of the students felt that the administration of CRLA had sold out on them.

At any rate, both CRLA and the Farm Workers Union felt that an outside investigation was necessary. They called on two California Assemblymen to ask the Attorney General of California for a probe of the high school and police department in Delano. The two Democrats, Leon Ralph of Los Angeles, and John Vasconcellos of San Jose, stated in their letter to Attorney General Thomas Lynch, "The potential for violence in Delano appears to be great. . . . We urge you to conduct an outside impartial investigation of the issues and do what you can to lessen community tension." In conclusion, the letter stated, "the [Delano] police have witnessed Anglo 'vigilantism' without interfering, and there is evidence of anti-union bias and also of racial and religious prejudice in the Delano Police Department."

A local Assemblyman, William Ketchum (Republican of Paso Robles), whose district includes Delano, immediately responded to the charge. He said that the call for an investigation was a "cheap political shenanigan" and that the trouble in Delano had been caused by "children supported by the usual community dissidents and counselled by a CRLA attorney." Meanwhile, the *Delano Record* pressed its attack on the students, and Mayor Loader publicly asked that the CRLA office in McFarland be closed down for involving itself in political issues.

I thought that the newspaper coverage was so one-sided that I sent the following letter to the *Fresno Bee*. It appeared in the Sunday edition.

"Editor of *The Bee*
"Sir:
"In the July 8 edition of *The Bee,* you ran a story about the activities of the California Rural Legal Assistance attorneys on behalf of striking students in Delano.

"The article gives full play to the feelings of city officials, police department spokesmen, and high school authorities. The reader is all but forced to conclude that these city institutions are blameless and the target of a smear campaign by a handful of agitators, students, and attorneys.

"The opinions of the striking students and of John Ortega [the CRLA attorney] were not solicited. The City of Delano charges that CRLA offices in McFarland should be closed since they confine themselves to labor cases. The Delano High School case is hardly a labor case but deals with the civil rights of young Chicanos—and these rights have been constantly violated by teachers and the police. I have seen matters grow worse in the three years I have been assistant pastor at Guadalupe Church in Delano.

"Students walked out of DHS on May 6 because of the discriminatory and racist attitudes they found there with the administration and teachers. Several teachers have made derogatory remarks about the culture and ethnic background of minority-group youngsters. Efforts to hire teachers of Mexican-American descent have been thwarted as well as special programs to aid Chicano students.

"From the beginning of the student strike, Chicano students have faced brutality and harassment from the Delano Police Department. On the evening of the graduation, policemen were stationed at the entrance to the school grounds. Connie Rangel, a pregnant 24-year-old woman who held a ticket to the graduation exercises, was denied entrance—and was brutally pushed to the ground by a police officer. When others protested, they were arrested. One woman was even Maced by police officers. Fifteen were arrested in all, twelve juveniles and three adults. Newspapers mentioned none of the facts about how the fracas started. They based their information on a biased and prejudiced police report.

"Attorney John Ortega has been criticized by CRLA Director Cruz Reynoso for being personally involved with the Chicano students. And why shouldn't he be, since no one else will come to their aid?

"I, for one, wish to commend the efforts of the McFarland CRLA attorneys. They have given some hope to the students when the police, the city officials, the welfare department, and the local newspaper mercilessly turned against them. Not only do I feel that CRLA should press its attack on Delano's educators and police, but outside agencies should make a thorough investigation of the entire situation. If nothing is done, it is very possible that the seething cauldron of repression and discontent will boil over. Then whose fault will it be?"

My comments must have hit dead center, because, within two days, I merited a special boxed-in section on the *Delano Record*'s front page:

"VILLAIN ROLE UNBECOMING

"Within the last few days this newspaper, referred to as 'the local press' has been mentioned by the CRLA as being prejudiced against Delano students of Mexican descent. Rev. Father Mark Day, in a letter to the Fresno Bee, stated that 'the local newspaper (and others) mercilessly turned against them' (the students involved in the fracas at the High School graduation) .

"Now, we have broad shoulders and we ordinarily would not bother to reply to such allegations and implications that this newspaper is prejudiced or merciless or unfair. We do so in this instance, however, to point out to our readers the technique constantly used by those who are seeking to further some cause in these troubled days, whether it be in Berkeley, at San Francisco State, or Santa Barbara. It would appear that someone has found a 'cause celebre' in Delano and seeks to inflate it.

"If you are not for them, you are automatically against them. If you do not plead their cause you are prejudiced.

"If you are a policeman trying to maintain order you are brutal. If you are a city councilman and do not join their ranks you are their enemy.

"It does not matter that you are trying to be fair. It does not matter that you are trying to be objective. It does not matter that you are seeking a neutral stance.

"You are against them.

"Because, you see, there must be an enemy. They must be put-upon. They must be the underdog. There has to be 'injustice' so they have something to yell about. Without a scapegoat they are nothing.

"Without a villain there can be no play.

"So when you read such charges as made by Rev. Father Mark Day, when the CRLA calls for an investigation naming the city police, city administrators, school administrators and newspapers as being prejudiced, brutal, et al, you will know that they have been selected to play the role of villain.

"We are quite worried, here at the 'local newspaper.'

"We don't think we play the villain very well."

There was also a vicious editorial article against the students by Mr. Noyes Alexander. He stated that the good citizens of Delano were fed up with the activities of the "misguided, misdirected youngsters, parading under the banner of the student strikers group."

Alexander separated the dissident group of students from the "good Mexicans" in town and accused the former of violent conduct and drug abuse. He concluded his column, calling for some good old-fashioned American vigilantism: "We believe it is up to the group whose good name is being besmirched by these young militants to take whatever action is necessary to maintain the excellent reputation it has enjoyed in Delano over the years."

The students lost their battle in the courts. Several of them told me that the police lied on the witness stand, and that most of the defense witnesses, who were high school students, were afraid to testify at the trial. The judge found the testimony of the police quite convincing.

Although charges were dropped against three of the juveniles, the rest were found guilty of a variety of charges, including assaulting an officer, resisting arrest, and disturbing the peace. They were given $50 fines and placed on probation.

The school took its revenge. The striking students were not promoted. Eloise and Dorothy Chavez were not permitted to graduate.

The Delano grape growers were undoubtedly a bit surprised when Cesar discussed the resolution of the high school strike as part of the negotiations with the grape industry. They were quite aware, however, that one of their fellow growers, Lido Sandrini, was also on the board of education and instrumental in opposing the Chicano students.

I feel that the ultimate outcome of the student strike will be productive for the students and the community. In the first place, the students are now aware of their rights and the political climate in Delano. And, now that UFWOC has won its long battle with the grape growers, it will be able to do some long-overdue organizing within the community. I am certain that the union will use its political muscle to help elect fair-minded city officials. I am sure that Delano will have a new police chief in the near future and that the bigots will be cleared out of the board of education.

The power that the union now wields has already created respect among many of the growers. As long as there are men like Cesar Chavez and his assistants, the union will use its influence responsibly. Meanwhile, things still look dismal on the west side, and much work needs to be done. It always helps, however, to have justice on one's side, and history.

[13]

At Last, the Bargaining Table

In the early spring of 1970, the leaves began appearing on the grapevines around Delano. An endless cycle repeated itself: birth, fruition, then the dead and cold of winter. Until recently, farm workers blended in with this scenario almost unnoticeably. People took their poverty, their hunger, and their dreary, hopeless existences for granted.

But in September, 1965, a cry for justice went forth from Delano. It was a cry of outrage and a cry of hope. The picket lines and the crowded strikers' meetings, the excitement in the air, spelled out a common longing: just because things were bad last year, and the year before, and the years before that—they did not have to be the same this year, or in the years to come.

The Delano strikers began a long, uphill fight in 1965. They began to chip away at the old foundations of the rural farm economy in order to build a new life for themselves and their families. It was an almost impossible task. They withdrew their labor from the vineyards and were replaced by foreign labor. They set up their picket lines and had them weakened by powerful injunctions. They pledged themselves to nonviolence and had to face violence and hatred from the grower agents and the institutionalized violence of corrupt courts, brutal policemen, and self-seeking politicians.

But, in spite of an endless stream of frustrating obstacles, victories have been won and despair has given way to hope. Farm workers unionized several ranches and have shouted "no" to the paternalism and exploitation of their bosses. They now have improved wages and working conditions. They have developed inspiring leadership among themselves on their ranches. They have learned the machinery of unionism: grievance procedures, negotiations, and the new sense of dignity and power every man needs in order to face the future.

The early victories of the farm workers came so swiftly that the strikers were caught off guard. We knew that the growers were taking a beating, but most of us thought that they would hold out for another year. The news of the breakthrough came during Easter time. It gave the season a special quality of jubilance. We knew that, if the major growers in the Coachella Valley were willing to begin negotiations, many others would soon follow.

The following chapter was written as UFWOC signed contract after contract in the spring and summer of 1970.

The weapon that ultimately forced the growers to the bargaining table was undoubtedly the grape boycott. With the price of grapes sagging and a dim forecast for a decent market, the struck growers were looking for ways to settle the dispute.

In early March, 1970, the newly appointed Catholic Bishops Ad Hoc Farm Labor Committee began to tour California, talking with both the growers and the union. The committee, headed by Auxiliary Bishop Joseph Don-

nelly, of Hartford, Connecticut, visited UFWOC's headquarters at Forty Acres and met with an assembly of
strikers. Donnelly brought with him four other members
of his committee: Bishop Humberto Madeiros, of Brownsville, Texas; Monsignor George Higgins, of the Department of Social Development, National Catholic Conference
in Washington, D.C.; Bishop Walter Curtis, of Bridgeport,
Connecticut; and Monsignor Roger Mahoney, of Fresno,
California.

The farm workers greeted the Bishops Committee with
mixed emotions. This was understandable, because many
of the workers and organizers had undergone bad experiences with bishops and priests during the course of the
struggle.

Bishop Madeiros commended Cesar for his efforts in
helping the working man and for his personal testimony
on behalf of nonviolence. George Higgins, the outspoken
secretary of the committee, also commended Cesar for his
"outstanding leadership." Speaking for himself, he promised to do everything possible to bring the growers to the
bargaining table, even if it meant endorsing the boycott.

In a subsequent report to the National Conference of
Catholic Bishops (NCCB), which had formed the committee, the following statement was made: "We visited 40
growers in one week, individually, and in small groups in
various parts of the Central Valley. Some were hostile, some
were friendly, and some were enthusiastic about the active
intervention of the Church in this dispute."

The committee's report to the NCCB disclosed that
Bishop Donnelly and Monsignor Higgins held meetings in
Washington, D.C., with the Secretary of Labor, the Under
Secretary of Labor, the Director of the Federal Mediation
and Conciliation Service, and with George Meany, President of the AFL-CIO. Finally, a joint session of growers
and union representatives met with the Bishops Committee
in Fresno.

Dolores Huerta told me just after the meeting that the

presence of the bishops lent seriousness and purpose to the gathering. The growers were rapidly made aware of the strong commitment that the Catholic Church had made toward the settlement of the dispute. Two California prelates, also members of the committee, were in attendance: Archbishop Timothy Manning, of Los Angeles, and Bishop Hugh Donohoe, of Fresno.

Manning was bishop of Fresno during some of the bitterest days of the dispute. He is a soft-spoken, shy man and wears a serious face. He once confided to me that he had learned a great deal from his experience with the grape strike. He suffered many personal conflicts, trying to be fair to both the growers and the workers. Like most of us who were brought up in a middle-class environment, Manning had a difficult time understanding the strike from the workers' point of view. He was made Archbishop of Los Angeles when Cardinal McIntyre retired in 1969. This, of course, did little to relieve his heavy burdens. His presence at the negotiations was invaluable. Archbishop Manning ordained me to the priesthood in 1965 at Santa Barbara. He was then Auxiliary Bishop of Los Angeles.

Bishop Hugh Donohoe was appointed Bishop of Fresno amid the protests of growers and their sympathizers. He had come to Delano from his diocese in Stockton in March, 1966, to testify on the rights of farm workers before a Senate Investigating Committee, headed by the late Senator Robert Kennedy.*

Speaking for the bishops of California he said, "Farm workers should not be looked upon as outside agitators if

---

* During this hearing, one of the most incisive repartees of the five-year-long struggle was made. Sheriff Thomas Galyen, of Kern County, was questioned by Kennedy as to why he had arrested a number of strikers one day during the harvest season. "They were *threatening* to break the law," he replied. At Kennedy's request, the sheriff repeated the sentence. Kennedy reminded the lawman that it is improper and illegal to arrest anyone for *threatening* to break the law. "I suggest we have a recess," Kennedy said. "Meanwhile I will ask the sheriff of Kern County to read through the Constitution of the United States of America."

they attempt to organize for their own self-defense." He added that their organizations should be protected by law and that it would be "unjust for grower organizations to strive to prevent their organization by reprisal" (*Central California Register,* March 17, 1966) . The grape growers never forgave Donohoe for this statement. The usual allegations of his being a communist sympathizer were made as well as his attempt to "mix politics with religion."

Donohoe has a pronounced Irish appearance. He has receding gray hair and is known for his quick wit and gruff manner. The latter, according to his close associates, is a defense for a native shyness.

One of his famous quips is frequently told at clerical gatherings on the West Coast. During the Vatican Council, a bishop in California solemnly vowed that he would never allow the use of the vernacular (English language) in the Masses conducted in his diocese. "Don't let it bother you," Donohoe remarked to some of his distraught colleagues. "He thinks that the vernacular is the married clergy!"

With the help of the Reverend Lloyd Saatjian of the First Methodist Church of Palm Springs, the Bishops Committee mediated negotiations with three Coachella Valley growers: Charles Freedman, David Freedman, and the Wonder Palms Farms. The first collective-bargaining contract covering table grapes in California was announced at a press conference held at the offices of the Archdiocese of Los Angeles. It set a pattern for subsequent agreements. The economic package agreed upon was $1.75 an hour plus 25 cents a box incentive during harvest time. In addition, 10 cents an hour was to be contributed to the Robert F. Kennedy Memorial Health and Welfare Fund. An average of 8 cents an hour (2 cents a box) for a special economic-development fund was also part of the pact.

The committee made a good showing in its first attempt at mediation. One of its crucial tests, insofar as UFWOC was concerned, was its attitude toward elections. The question of elections would arise again and again in subsequent months. UFWOC had offered the grape growers elections for the first three years of the strike. At the end of this time, the union withdrew its election offer and demanded outright recognition. During those three years, growers had intimidated the workers and created an unfair climate for elections. They had also conspired together, falsifying labels on grape boxes and contributing to a common war chest in order to break the union. When the international boycott of grapes became effective, growers called upon Governor Ronald Reagan to bail them out of their troubles. Reagan, who had always been opposed to elections and was extremely hostile to the very existence of UFWOC, took up the clarion call for "democracy" and chided Chavez for not agreeing to elections. Reagan later contradicted himself, when he rejected UFWOC's pleas for elections in the Salinas Valley lettuce strike.

As the negotiations began, the negotiator for the growers attempted to use the Bishops Committee for his own ends. Unaware of Donnelly's many years of experience as a skilled mediator in labor relations, he asked the bishop to petition Chavez to accept elections. Donnelly was keenly aware of the mileage the growers could get from Chavez's refusal. The negotiator was undoubtedly a bit embarrassed when the bishop chided him for attempting to use him in that fashion.

In its report to the NCCB, the Bishops Committee was quite frank. "Amazing to us was the scanty communications which the growers have with one another and [the] almost total lack of communications they have with the union . . . growers in the Delano area have never met Chavez. . . . Although the growers are convinced that their workers are very happy and do not want a union, those workers we talked to felt quite the contrary."

The latter remarks were no doubt directed at the bishops' opposition in the Catholic right wing, personified by the conservative weekly newspaper *Twin Circle*. Monsignor Higgins, in his own nationally syndicated weekly column, had been carrying on a long-standing editorial feud with *Twin Circle*'s editor, Father Daniel Lyons, S.J., and its "farm-labor correspondent," Father Cletus Healy, also a Jesuit.

During the course of the negotiations between Chavez and the grape growers, Lyons editorialized that farm workers did not want Chavez's union, that growers had been immorally coerced into signing, and that Chavez had profited from arson and violence perpetrated against the growers.

Bishop Donnelly retaliated, calling Lyons's comments on the grape strike "the dirtiest kind of reporting I have ever read." Donnelly added, "Knowing at first hand what is now going on, it is incredible to read this mishmash of untruths, deceptions, innuendos, and inaccuracies. . . . Rather than inflict on its readers this libelous report, it would serve a constructive purpose if it tried to find the facts and attempted to promote understanding and cooperation between the parties to the ultimate good of both the growers and the workers."

In August, 1970, Lyons was forced to resign as editor and publisher of *Twin Circle*. The action was taken by two of the paper's board chairmen, Archbishop Robert J. Dwyer, of Portland, Oregon, and Patrick Frawley, Jr., a multimillionaire right-wing industrialist. Lyons's anti-union and anti-Chavez editorials and his heavy criticism of the Bishops Committee precipitated the action. Dwyer commented, "Patrick Frawley and I are deeply disturbed over Father Lyons's unfair criticism of Los Angeles Archbishop Timothy Manning and the other members of the ad hoc committee."

Another significant breakthrough in the vineyards came on April 11, 1970. Keene and Cecil Larsan, grape growers in the Coachella Valley, had toured the nation saying that their workers did not want Chavez's union. The Larsans claimed that they would agree to an election to prove it. Chavez made an exception to his stand on elections to prove a point. Elections, supervised by the Reverend Saatjian, of Palm Springs, and Monsignor Mahoney, of Fresno, were held at the two Larsan ranches. Workers voted almost unanimously for representation by UFWOC: 152 to 2.

The first major breakthrough among the Delano growers occurred on May 21, 1970. After long and tedious negotiations, two major grape growers completed collective-bargaining contracts with UFWOC: Bruno Dispoto and the Bianco Fruit Corporation. At the press conference, held in Fresno, Bishop Donnelly announced that members of his committee took part as observers and informal mediators during the negotiations.

Both Anthony Bianco and Bruno Dispoto were talkative during the news conference. "Unionization is here to stay, and it is just part of the American way of life," Bianco said. "I felt that it was time to stop thinking with our hearts and start thinking with our heads. With our present settlement, we can go anywhere we want with our grapes, and we can do a better job."

Dispoto, a sharply dressed man and a longtime foe of UFWOC, stated, "I am firmly convinced at this point that Cesar Chavez and his union are here to stay. The boycott has hampered our operation. I was not going to tolerate another year of insecurity. I spoke to my workers, and their attitude was that there would be no problems if we began to negotiate."

Cesar handled the press with his usual expertise. He announced that strike fever had taken hold of farm workers in California. He was not exaggerating. Strikes were about to start in the melon fields of Calexico, the vegetable fields of Santa Maria and Salinas, and the citrus groves of Fillmore. Rumblings were also evident in the tree-fruit industries near Fresno and just south of Delano.

When reporters asked about mechanization on the farms, Cesar answered, "Our union is not against automation and machines. The only difference we have with the growers on this question is that we feel technology was given to man by God not only for the privileged few, but to everyone. The dispute is not that machines are coming in. The dispute is that the workers should also be the direct beneficiaries of technology and mechanization." His answer was simple, yet unusual. Most of us are so brainwashed by our technological values that we look upon mechanization as the unilateral tool of management or the product of blind fate. Cesar has seen the cruel displacement of the farm worker by machinery for years. His only desire is that human beings be given primary consideration.

On June 10, another major breakthrough was announced. One of the largest farms in California, owned by Hollis B. Roberts, signed a collective-bargaining agreement with UFWOC. As in the case of several other ranches, the workers on Roberts Farms had decided to strike and came to UFWOC's offices for advice and direction. Roberts faced several walkouts and was willing to begin talks.

The June 10 agreement was similar to the grape agreements. The press conference was again chaired by Bishop Donnelly, who commended the cooperation that prevailed throughout the negotiations. Hollis Roberts, a heavy-set gentleman farmer from Texas, drawled his approval of Cesar. He stated, "Cesar Chavez and his negotiators dealt with me in good faith and guaranteed me the right to let me run my own business."

Jerry Cohen, UFWOC's directing attorney told me that Roberts looked like Sidney Greenstreet with a Texas drawl. "When he talks," Jerry said, "he bites his cigar with his teeth, throws his head back, and looks at you through the narrow slits of his eyelids."

Cesar tells the following anecdote about Roberts: "Hollis came up to me during the negotiations, and put his arm around my shoulders. Hollis said, 'I know, Cesar, that you love the Lord's poor people, and I love the Lord's poor people. I was wonderin' if we could do something for them. If you could cancel out that initiation fee for the workers [first three months dues in advance], why, you would stand as tall as an oil derrick in my mind.' I answered him, 'Hollis, you would stand as tall as *two* oil derricks if you would guarantee to hire those forty-six strikers you fired during the strike on your farms!' "

Roberts is one of the largest fruit and nut growers in California. He owns and manages 46,798 acres of land from his headquarters in McFarland, ten miles south of Delano. His nurseries contain over 400,000 young trees, and his employees exceed 4,500.

By the end of June, farm workers and their supporters knew that a landslide was taking place—the growers were literally standing in line to negotiate with UFWOC and have the black eagle stamped on their grape boxes. The boycott had become so effective that the struck grapes became more unpopular than the black plague. Henry Reider, of the Coachella Valley Imperial Distributors, a shipper with thirty-three grower clients, complained that he could not move 11,000 boxes of grapes before he negotiated with UFWOC. As soon as he signed with the union, he sold every box to eastern markets within two days.

On June 26, over 11,500 acres of grapes were added to UFWOC coverage in four contracts signed with two companies: the Tenneco Corporation, one of the largest conglomerates in the United States, and S. A. Camp, a huge San Joaquin Valley grower. Tenneco has three farming corporation subsidiaries: The Kern Land Farm Company, Heggblade & Marguleas of Coachella, and Rancho El Dorado, of Phoenix, Arizona. The S. A. Camp Company, of Shafter, California, now farms part of the old Di Giorgio land near Arvin and has bought the Pete Divizich ranch near Ducor in Tulare County—a 6,000-acre spread.

Chavez had begun to mobilize an international boycott of Tenneco products. This seemed to hasten the collective-bargaining process.

Bargaining sessions are often long, drawn-out meetings. The bulk of the time is spent in caucusing and discussions that last until the wee hours of the morning.

When I arrived at the Casa Royale Motel in Bakersfield one early afternoon, UFWOC's bargaining team was finishing its sessions with representatives of Tenneco and S. A. Camp. The atmosphere was cordial. The spokesman for the growers was a pleasant, middle-aged attorney by the name of Lee Shaw. Shaw entered the meeting room alone with a busied look on his face, puffing on his pipe. He addressed Cesar, who was sitting with his arms folded over the back of a chair. "Cesar," he said, "I want to get these wine-picking rates straight." Bill Kircher, the national director of organization for the AFL-CIO, joined the conversation, which soon shifted to another topic: Who was to supervise the ratification elections? The union suggested the clergy in the person of the Bishops Committee. Shaw preferred other mediators, but Kircher assured him that the Catholic Church was not monolithically lined up on Chavez's side. In fact, he stated, the bishops had just been run out of the Imperial Valley by growers when they attempted to mediate the melon strike. The Catholic clergy of the area had supported the growers' position. Shaw conferred with the growers, and they agreed to let the Bishops Committee supervise the ratification elections. The negotiations concluded like the final act of a play. The representatives of the growers and the union had one last conference together and shook hands, sealing the pact.

Within a half hour, Cesar began another set of negotiations with another set of growers, the Armenians from the Arvin and Lamont area. This was the area in which John Steinbeck lived and worked when he wrote *The Grapes of Wrath*. As the meeting began, Cesar greeted Gene Nalbandian, one of the growers. Nalbandian, like Cesar, has an ailing back. Cesar sympathized with him and made sure he had comfortable seating at the bargaining table.

The negotiations moved rapidly. By 7:00 P.M., Cesar was addressing a cheering strikers' meeting at Filipino Hall in Delano, announcing the terms of the recent victories.

The face of the union leader was drooping with fatigue. He gave a progress report on the melon strikes that Manuel and Richard Chavez were conducting in Calexico and Yuma, Arizona. He also announced that a citrus strike was under way in Ventura County.

Cesar adjourned the meeting early. He shook hands with a few well-wishers and slipped out the back door of the union hall. He had just finished another round, but the real heavyweights, the Delano growers, were next in line.

[14]

Fillmore:
A Strike Is Revived

During a lull in the negotiations with the grape growers in the latter part of July, 1970, I accompanied Cesar on a trip to Santa Barbara. We went there to inspect a printing press that the Franciscans were to donate to the farm-workers union. The highway to Santa Barbara passes through Bakersfield and south over the Tejon Pass of the Tehachapi Mountains. Cesar was in a talkative mood, as we drove through the sweltering heat of the valley floor. He began to relate some experiences from his trip around the country the previous fall. He laughed as he told about his visit to Capitol Hill. Senator Ralph Yarborough had given Cesar and his traveling companions a special welcome in the Senate Office Building. Cesar had delivered a speech from the top of a desk.

Tight security was placed on Cesar at this time, and everyone was a bit worried because a woman stood at the doorway, saying that she had "a message from God for

Mr. Chavez." Cesar was whisked out the back door and did not realize until he was in his car that Yarborough had placed a $100 bill in his hand as a donation to the strike fund.

After we had inspected the printing presses in Santa Barbara, we immediately headed for home in Delano. We stopped in Fillmore and learned that a citrus strike was just about to begin.

It was late at night when we arrived at the home of Benjamin Aparicio in Fillmore. I was half asleep, and Cesar had to nudge me to keep me awake as I drove the last few miles into town. Fillmore is surrounded by Sunkist packing sheds and the coastal mountains, which skirt the Santa Clarita Valley. Ben Aparicio had been organizing the area's farm workers ever since their first walkout early in July. He is the eldest son of a family of eight, which immigrated from Jerez, Zacatecas, Mexico, in 1961. He had just finished his second year on a scholarship at Moor Park Junior College, where he had led his track team to the state finals.

Ben's older sister Manuela, a tall, attractive girl who had spent two years in a convent, was typing a stencil for a leaflet when Cesar and two of his bodyguards, Manuel Uranday and Ray Olivos entered the house ahead of me. She served us *pan dulce* (Mexican sweet bread) and coffee.

The other organizers from Fillmore arrived, and Cesar began to discuss the citrus strike, impressing on the young men the need for a highly organized effort. "Unless you hit a company like Sunkist with a big strike and a big boycott, you will never get anywhere," Cesar said. "Even in the most effective strike, you can only count on 15 per cent of the people to support you solidly. The other 85 per cent? Most will sympathize with you, but they will either leave the area or go back to work. Some will be unwilling to make any sacrifices. Some will sell out, and a certain number will become what we call hard-core scabs."

The power of the citrus industry had been demonstrated in 1941, when a strike was crushed by the Associated Farmers, the Farm Bureau, and the State Chamber of Commerce. Farm workers had been ejected from company housing and labor camps and had to live like animals in tents and under bridges. Pickets had been arrested, and tightly organized grower groups vowed to fight to the finish. They recruited labor from all possible sources to replace the strikers.

George Meany, president of the AFL-CIO, was on the scene in those days. He reported that the family of Charles Collins Teague then controlled a large percentage of the 22,500 acres of citrus in the area. "The Ventura County lemon pickers lead lives that have been likened to slaves," he said. He quoted Teague as saying, "We cannot and must not accede to the union's demands. It would be better for us to let the fruit on the trees drop to the ground than to grant their demands." Teague had his way. Veterans from the 1941 strike relate that the whole Santa Clarita Valley was blanketed by the stench of rotting lemons and oranges for months. Millions of dollars were lost, and so was the strike.

Ben Aparicio and his colleagues were listening intently to what Cesar was saying. I began to fall asleep, catching a few comments here and there. "When you take on the big farms, you have to make every minute, every penny, every person count. You can't do things haphazardly, or you will lose everything," Cesar said. "A strike which is not well organized is a *huelga loca*. Everyone is all fired up, but without clear-cut goals, or methods, or leadership and discipline. You have to make sure your leadership is prepared. There are many pitfalls which a leader can fall into. The pressures get fierce when a strike is on. There are many temptations. You have to organize your wives and families so that they become an asset and not a liability in the struggle. There will be a lot of *sangre, sudor, y lagrimas* [blood, sweat, and tears], but, in the long run, it will be worth it."

One of the organizers, Tony Granados, asked what groups they might contact for help. Cesar answered that strikers should ask for help from every possible source. "When you are on strike," Cesar said, "there is only one class of people, the kind that help you. Don't segregate yourselves as one race. On the other hand, don't let any person, or group of persons, try to tell you what to do. You are always the boss, here, don't forget that!"

I dozed off to sleep. When I awoke, Cesar asked me to stay in Fillmore and help with the strike. More organizers and UFWOC attorney Chuck Farnsworth would come down the next day from Delano.

Ben woke me at 4:30 the next morning. Some forty workers were milling about in front of the Aparicio home in the predawn darkness. We walked down the Southern Pacific tracks to the packing sheds of the Fillmore Citrus Association. We were to picket the entrance of the packing sheds, since none of the workers were picking in the orchards. They had agreed to stay away from work. I walked with Manuela and one of her younger sisters. I asked Manuela how Ben became involved with the strike. "Ben has worked in the citrus ever since he was twelve years old," she said. "He used to tell me about the frustration he saw in the faces of the men as they came home from work on the company trucks after a long day's work. He would tell me, 'No wonder they hang around the bars and get drunk. No wonder some of them take their anger out on their wives and children. They see no way out of the trap they are in.'"

A group of more than forty men, women, and children carried picket signs that read: "We Demand a Union!," "Fillmore Citrus Workers on Strike," and "No Contract, No Work." I advised Ben to appoint a person in each picket line to keep order and explain the rules of the picket line to the strikers: no returning insults to passers-by, no profane or obscene language, no blocking of traffic, no littering, and so on.

Manuela began to distribute the leaflet she had made the evening before. It announced that workers were being badly treated, poorly paid, cheated, and medically neglected by the Fillmore and Piru Citrus Associations. It concluded, "We demand union recognition, better housing, better communications between workers and employers, better wages, and work by contract before we work again in the orchards. We have united and our brother Cesar Chavez is supporting and helping us. *Viva la Huelga!!!*"

Later on during the day, I accompanied Ben and some organizers in a meeting with the chief of police in Fillmore and a representative from the Ventura County sheriff's department. Chief Reid Hunt is an obese man in his fifties, with a gaudy silver belt-buckle with his initials inlaid in gold. He reminded me of Rod Steiger's portrayal of the Sheriff in the movie *In the Heat of the Night*.

With a hint of paternalism, Hunt told Ben that he had received good reports about his work with the youth in the area (Ben had been coaching sports at the boys club). But he warned that he wanted no trouble. He added that, if any of his officers stepped out of line, Ben should contact him. He would in turn contact Ben if the strikers were involved in any disturbances. Hunt said that he had been assigned to the 1941 strike as a rookie policeman. He boasted that there had been relatively few incidents at that time. As we left his office, one of the Chicano community leaders whispered to me that the chief failed to mention that the 1941 strike had been thoroughly busted. "The strikers didn't even have a chance to open their mouths," he told me, with a sad look on his face.

Cesar returned to Fillmore a few days later and addressed the strikers from the front porch of Ben Aparicio's house. After he spoke, the workers recounted to him their grievances: Growers were charging high rents at the labor camps—$3.50 a day for each man. The food was miserable and the living quarters crowded. Workers were being cheated on the picking rates. Ben Aparicio had been fired when he complained about this. No toilets were provided in the orchards. The family housing was in serious disrepair. If a worker complained about it, he was fired. "The association promises us medical attention," stated Paulo Izquierdo, president of the Santa Paula local of the Farm Workers. "But it turns out to be a joke. Recently a man fell off a ladder on the job. He tore a gash in his body. They stitched him up and put him back on the job in one day. He developed a horrible abscess. They gave him $50 and told him to go back to Mexico and get cured."

Several developments took place in the next few days. Approximately 150 grower-members of the Citrus Association met and decided to meet all the demands of the workers, except the recognition of UFWOC. But the workers were skeptical, since growers still made no mention of what they would be paying the pickers. Neither did they guarantee amnesty to workers who had gone on strike. The workers had a rally in which they unanimously voted to continue the strike, demanding recognition of UFWOC as their sole bargaining agent.

Just before the rally, an interesting and comical incident took place when Ben Aparicio and I tried to get a meeting place for the workers. The local Catholic pastor was on vacation but gave explicit orders not to let the strikers use his parish hall. (We later found out that the church owned some citrus acreage.) Ben and I stopped at a gas station to make a phone call. As I began to take a drink of water, I heard three middle-aged women speaking in a raucous fashion nearby. One of them kept repeating, "Chavez has no business here in Fillmore. We want no part of him."

Another retorted, "They're all communists, you know.

I read in a pamphlet that there are thirty communists who work right along with Chavez."

The scene reminded me of the witches from *Macbeth*, cackling around their boiling cauldron.

"They're just a bunch of troublemakers as far as I'm concerned," the third woman added.

Just as I finished taking my drink of water, I heard one of them remark, "I saw in the paper last night that they have a priest with them." She spit out the word "priest" as though it were poison.

"I don't believe it," another rejoined, in a staged voice.

"It's true! It's true!," she shouted. "It's right in the Ventura *Star-Free Press*!"

At this point, clad in a sport shirt and black pants, I slowly walked over to the ladies and asked them, "What's this I hear about a priest being with the strikers?"

The trio eyed me inquisitively as one of them explained what she had read in the paper.

I nodded in negative dismay and solemnly stated with a smirk, "What will they think of next?"

Moments later, the women saw Ben and me together as we left the filling station. They became openly hostile. "Why don't you go back to Mexico, you damn wetback?" they shouted at Ben. "Why don't you go to Vietnam and fight for your country like a man?"

One of the women came close to the car, her eyes bulging with hatred. "You lousy bastard," she screamed. "You've never worked a day in your life!"

I slowed my car to a stop and told one of the women, "He's not a troublemaker. He's just trying to help his people."

It was too late. They were completely out of control. The women were screaming anathemas at us. Beside them, a mechanic paused from his tune-up job. He stared at all of us in confusion. As we drove down the street, Ben and I had a good laugh. "It's a good thing they aren't armed," I remarked. "They'd be dangerous."

The next morning, a television crew from Santa Barbara arrived with the rumor that the growers would accept elections. Cesar contacted two grower spokesmen by phone. They seemed vague about the election offer and referred him to a third party. His name was Ivan McDaniels, an elderly attorney for the Ventura County Citrus Association. He had played a major role in putting down the 1941 strike. Liberals in the area refer to him as Ivan the Terrible. He must have been surprised to discover Cesar Chavez at the other end of a telephone conversation. Cesar explained the workers' desire for an election.

"I hope you're not planning another boycott," McDaniels said. "You've done a lot of disservice to our country by your grape boycott."

Cesar tensed up with shock and anger. "You're *kidding!*" he shot back at McDaniels. "You're *kidding!*"

"No, I'm not kidding, Mr. Chavez," McDaniels replied.

"We've done a lot more than anyone else to eradicate poverty in this country, and you *know* it!" Cesar said, emphatically.

McDaniels gave no definite answer to the election offer. I later learned that, in 1939, he had led the growers' attack on strikers in Lindsay, California. They were being paid $2 a day in the orange harvest. In the 1941 strike, he served the eviction notices on the citrus strikers in Ventura County. Whole families were forced into tent cities built along the river bank.

The next week brought with it a postponement of further strike action. The workers needed enough resources and organization in order to deal effectively with the multi-million-dollar citrus industry.

Meanwhile, all eyes were trained on Delano. Rumors had it that the twenty-six major grape growers had decided to enter the twentieth century by signing collective-bargaining agreements with the United Farm Workers Organizing Committee.

UNITED FARM WORKERS ORGANIZING COMMITTEE, AFL-CIO

By _[signature]_____   By _____

_[signature]_____   _____

_____   _____

_____   _____

GIUMARRA VINEYARDS, CORP   NICK BOZANICH, JR.

By _[signature]_____   By _[signature]_____
   "Company"   "Company"

GEORGE A. LUCAS & SONS   VINCENT B. ZANINOVICH & SONS INC.

By _[signature]_____   By _[signature]_____
   "Company"   "Company"

DAN TUDOR & SONS   GENE RADOVICH & SONS

By _____   By _[signature]_____
   "Company"   "Company"

STEPHEN PAVICH & SONS   JOHN PAGLIARULO INC

By _[signature]_____   By _[signature]_____
   "Company"   "Company"

MORRIS FRUIT COMPANY   ANTON CARATAN & SON

By _[signature]_____   By _[signature]_____
   "Company"   "Company"

M. CARATAN INC.   SANDRINI BROS.

By _[signature]_____   By _[signature]_____
   "Company"   "Company"

PANDOL & SONS   SAM BARBIC

By _[signature]_____   By _[signature]_____
   "Company"   "Company"

JACK & MARION J. RADOVICH   VINCENT V. ZANINOVICH & SONS

By _[signature]_____   By _[signature]_____
   "Company"   "Company"

MID STATE HORTICULTURE CO. INC.   JOHN DULCICH & SONS

By _[signature]_____   By _[signature]_____
   "Company"   "Company"

LOUIS CARIC & SONS   MARLIN BROTHERS

By _[signature]_____   By _[signature]_____
   "Company"   "Company"

A & N ZANINOVICH   JAKE J. CESARE & SONS

By _[signature]_____   By _[signature]_____
   "Company"   "Company"

FRANK A. LUCICH CO. INC.   JASMINE VINEYARDS

By _[signature]_____   By _[signature]_____
   "Company"   "Company"

JACK G. ZANINOVICH FARMS   M.B ZANINOVICH, INC.

By _[signature]_____   by _[signature]_____
   "Company"   "Company"

[15]

Victoria en Delano!

I was working in the office of *El Malcriado* on a hot, dusty morning in late July when I heard the news. Cesar and his negotiating team were about to begin formal negotiations with the major grape growers of Delano. I grabbed my notebook and walked to UFWOC's main office building, which sits on the south corner of Forty Acres. Cesar, Dolores Huerta, Larry Itliong, and Jerry Cohen were boarding a car driven by Bill Kircher. I asked if *El Malcriado* could cover the historic occasion. "Sure," Cesar said. "Follow us."

A half hour later, we arrived at the Holiday Inn Motel in Bakersfield. The interior of the Holiday Inn is a compromise between Spanish Colonial and Mexican Rancho architecture—a compromise, I might add, that did not succeed very well.

The collective-bargaining sessions were to be held in the Isabella Room, painted and decorated in deep red. Three tables equipped with water pitchers and glasses were arranged in the shape of a horseshoe. UFWOC's negotiating team faced the grower representatives and

their chief negotiator, Phillip Feick. At the head table at
the far corner of the room, sat Bishop Joseph Donnelly,
flanked by his two assistants, Monsignor George Higgins
and Monsignor Roger Mahoney.

Bill Kircher was the first to speak. He is a giant of a
man who commands attention when he speaks. His voice
is deep, determined, and resonant. The atmosphere was
somewhat tense. Both sides had built up a reserve of hostility and antagonism which Kircher alluded to in his
introductory remarks. It was evident, however, that the
growers were extremely ill at ease.

Kircher stressed the need for a total peace between
both sides. He pointed out that the union was aware of
its responsibilities and was willing to live up to its duties
and obligations. "But we want total peace, or no peace
with the industry," he stated. "We will never really love
each other, but we can try to understand one another. We
want to arrive at this point, if and when a contract is
signed."

Feick spoke next. He stressed that the growers had
reached the same conclusion. "Obstructionism on our part
can only result in a nonproductive arrangement. We are
here to bring about as total a peace as possible. What we
offer you may be unacceptable. What you offer us may be
unpalatable. But we are here to work out a settlement
acceptable to both sides." Feick began to recite the litany
of the ills that beset the agricultural industry. There was
a marked contrast between his style and that of Kircher's.
Kircher, a former newspaperman and a veteran negotiator, economized his words. His sentences were well
thought out, and he rarely opened himself to illogical
statements or vulnerable positions. Feick spoke in long,
boring monologues, full of verbal padding and with few
breathing spaces. He did succeed, however, in guarding
the growers' position.

Kircher alluded to the troubles at Delano High School
and said that community problems were deeply related

to the settlement of the strike. "We are not intent on building any contractual ghettos. We intend to upgrade life in the entire community." Kircher also alluded to the profiteering on food and rent that takes place at labor camps and said that it had to stop.

On Feick's left sat John Giumarra, Jr., the son of the largest table-grape grower in the world. John is an articulate young attorney. He had engaged in several legal battles with UFWOC since the strike had started at his father's ranches east of Bakersfield and near Delano. The young Giumarra is a graduate of Stanford. He was well dressed in a sport jacket with gold buttons, a blue shirt, and ornate tie and cufflinks To the right of Feick sat two Delano growers, Louis Lucas and Louis Caratan. Both were serious faced and dressed in sport clothes.

During a recess, Cesar asked me about Lucas and Caratan. I smiled, because I felt that Cesar should have known that a slight communication barrier existed between myself and the growers. "You ought to know better than I how friendly or hostile they are," I taunted Cesar. "You've been on strike with them for the last five years!" Cesar threw up his hands and tilted his head, somewhat in impish bewilderment.

Later in the afternoon, UFWOC submitted its wage proposal to the growers. A series of caucuses and joint sessions took place, but communications continued at a slow pace.

Two days later, after Feick had consulted with more Delano grape growers on the wage proposals, another joint session was held at the Holiday Inn. At this meeting, several Delano strikers joined the sessions as observers. Also present for the first time was Martin Zaninovich, president of the South Central Farmers Committee. The committee had been formed in Delano at the beginning of the strike to combat the effectiveness of UFWOC propaganda and habitually made rash statements until it became evident that UFWOC was definitely on the winning side. In the last year of the struggle, the committee refrained from any diatribes against the union. I always regarded this as a sign that the "Delano bunch" were thinking of negotiating with the union.

Several waiting periods took place as the growers examined UFWOC's proposals and counterproposals. During these periods, we had our own meetings or simply exchanged banter about past experiences during the struggle. Jerry Cohen discussed a moving scene that took place at the packing sheds of the Sam Andrews melon ranch two weeks previously. A growers' attorney was coaxing some workers to cross our picket line. The workers were old-time dust-bowlers, who had seen many farm-labor strikes in the past. One of the men shouted back at the attorney, "I've been a fruit tramp for thirty goddam years, fella, and I ain't never crossed a goddam picket line. And I ain't gonna cross no goddam picket line now!"

"It looked like a scene right out of Steinbeck's *In Dubious Battle*," Jerry said, excitedly. "The attorney *pleaded* with the workers, telling them they would make $100 a day if they worked. But not one of them crossed the line."

A week later, the final phases of the negotiations were under way at a Delano motel. After some preliminary discussions, a joint session took place between twenty-six Delano grape growers and UFWOC's bargaining team. The meeting was held at St. Mary's grammar school auditorium in Delano. Since the services of the bishops and Feick were no longer considered necessary, John Giumarra, Jr., and Jerry Cohen mediated the talks between the two parties.

When I arrived at the grammar school, the discussion revolved around the issue of rehiring the strikers on a priority basis. Cesar had attended a previous session but was called to other business, leaving the final stages to Jerry Cohen, Dolores Huerta, Marshall Ganz, Richard Chavez, and Irwin De Shettler, an AFL-CIO negotiator.

From the time I entered the hall, I noticed that a few

of the growers, including Martin Zaninovich, had been eying me intently. I passed this over as an innate paranoia on my part, but I soon found out there was some basis to their preoccupation with me. During the morning session, the two priests from St. Mary's had joined the discussions, seated with the growers. To Cesar and his negotiating team, the sight of the priests with the growers was a powerful symbol of where the sympathies of these two men of the cloth had been during the five-year-long struggle. The pastor, an elderly Irishman, had at times militantly campaigned against UFWOC. At the request of the union, the priests left the hall.

It is understandable, I guess, that my arrival at the hall a few hours later was not exactly heralded by the growers with open arms. Martin Zaninovich motioned to John Giumarra to have me ejected. During a recess, I overheard Giumarra telling Jerry Cohen that the priest "had to go." Dolores Huerta intervened on my behalf.

"He's not a third party," she said. "He's the editor of our newspaper, *El Malcriado*. He has just as much right to be here as any of us. He'll stay!"

Giumarra walked over to Zaninovich and whispered a few words to him. The latter shrugged his shoulders in resignation. Giumarra sat down to resume the negotiations. I knew I was *in*. I later thanked Dolores for her help.

The remainder of the bargaining sessions moved rapidly. Discussion centered on wage proposals, the administration of labor camps, the unionization of other crops such as lettuce and tomatoes, and the high school issue, which was never settled at the bargaining table.

At one point during the discussion, grower Steve Pandol stated that he wanted a guaranteed work force for his lettuce crop. I was amused by the humanitarian tones in his voice when he complained of being forced to plow under his lettuce for lack of a work force. "This would be a shame," he said, "since there are so many starving people in the world." If the Pandols were so concerned about poverty and undernourishment, they should have negotiated with UFWOC five years previously. They have remained the staunchest foes of the union and are still active in the right-to-work movement in California.

The growers were beginning to get restless and wanted to finish the negotiations in the early evening. "Let's get this thing moving," said John Giumarra, Sr. "I'm no expert in labor relations, but I'm sure we don't need any of this all-night marathon stuff." Giumarra, a short, stocky, olive-complexioned man in his fifties, ran his hand through his gray hair as he remarked to Dolores Huerta that the Sicilians had given the farm workers a good run for their money.

The final discussion covered the framing of the contract in its final stages, the signing, and the ratification elections on each ranch. The meeting was finally adjourned, and the growers shook hands with UFWOC's negotiating team. Afterwards, I approached Martin Zaninovich and John Giumarra, Jr., in order to shake their hands.

"I thought we might bury all the hatchets, Martin," I said, extending my hand.

Zaninovich said calmly, forcing a smile, "Well, Father, I don't really know if there are any *hatchets* to bury," he said.

"You have been a rather controversial guy, at that," interjected Giumarra, and he also shook my hand.

With that, I bid them good night and told them that I would see them at the press conference the next morning.

The signing of the Delano growers was a gala occasion. Busloads of strikers and volunteers arrived from San Francisco and Los Angeles where they had been working on the grape boycott. More than 500 people jammed the hall at UFWOC's headquarters at Forty Acres. The front of the hall was a maze of reporters, TV cameras, and recording gear. Cameramen and reporters fought with each other for a good vantage point. Long cloth banners adorned the interior of the hall. On them were colorful inscriptions in English and Spanish, such as, "First Relieve the Needy, Then Ask Questions," and "For the Hungry, *Wait* Is a Hard Word."

Augie Lira, formerly of the *Teatro Campesino,* and I began to sing strike songs with the workers as we waited for the press conference to begin. After each song we shouted, *Viva la Huelga! Viva la Causa! Viva Cesar Chavez!*

When the twenty-six Delano growers and their families entered the hall, the workers began to shout *Huelga!* in unison. We then began to sing *De Colores,* another song of the strike. The Bishops Committee representatives entered next, followed by Cesar and UFWOC assistant director Larry Itliong. They were flanked by the union's vice-presidents, Dolores Huerta, Phillip Veracruz, and Julio Hernandez.

Cesar was the first to speak, stating that the signing was a proof of the power of nonviolence. He thanked the supporters of the grape boycott throughout the United States and commended the sacrifices of the Delano strikers. "Ninety-five per cent of the strikers lost their homes and cars. But I think that, in losing their worldly possessions in order to serve the poor, they found themselves."

Referring to the five-year-long battle, Cesar said, "The strike has been long and costly for both the employers and the strikers. The material losses can never be regained, but I think that, despite our unfortunate experiences, we have created the foundation upon which we hope to build a very good working relationship with the grower community in Delano."

Larry Itliong briefly recounted the sad history of the Filipino farm workers. "But today is the beginning of a new era on behalf of farm workers," he said, "hopefully for better conditions and a better way of life for our people."

John Giumarra, Jr., began his remarks with a trite

aphorism about a journey of a thousand miles beginning with one step. He added, "The power of the union and the power of the industry can now work together so that both the farmer and the worker can reap the benefits."

The final wage package agreed upon was $1.80 an hour plus 20 cents a box during the harvest season. This was to be increased to $1.95 in 1971 and to $2.05 in 1972. Ten cents an hour would be contributed to the Robert F. Kennedy Health and Welfare Fund. Two cents a box would go to a special economic development fund planned to help workers face automation and similar problems. The three-year agreement followed the pattern set by the other table-grape contracts, including a hiring hall, protective clauses on the use of pesticides, and a ban on lockouts and strikes during harvest time.

Even as Chavez spoke at the press conference, the news broke that the Teamsters were busy signing back-door or "sweetheart" agreements with some 200 vegetable growers in the Salinas and Santa Maria valleys. Without resting so much as an afternoon, Cesar left for Salinas with the intention of remaining there until his union won contracts with the Growers and Shippers associations. The farm workers of the area were to welcome him as a friend. To them he was known as the man who had fasted almost to death's door on behalf of nonviolence and the man who had conquered the powerful grape growers in Delano.

[16]

Salinas:
Reds, Lettuce Alone!

———————

Even before the victorious signings in Delano, lettuce workers had notified Cesar about the Teamsters' organizing drive in the Salinas and Santa Maria valleys. UFWOC organizers immediately began to sign authorization cards with farm workers in those areas. There was no doubt as to the loyalties of the workers. Growers knew that the field hands wanted the Chavez union but quickly negotiated contracts with the Teamsters. Grower spokesmen openly admitted that they considered the Teamsters the lesser of two evils.

By early August, 1970, UFWOC had obtained the signatures of the majority of the 10,000 workers in the two valleys. The Teamsters had only signed a few hundred cards and began to confine their activities to goon-squad tactics against UFWOC.

I asked some of the workers about their personal feelings in the matter. Angie Lopez, a twenty-five-year-old packinghouse and cold-storage worker had left her job under a Teamster contract and joined the field workers' strike. "The Teamsters never showed any interest in us until Cesar came here," she told me. "Now they say they represent our interests. Every time we had a problem and needed their help in the past, they couldn't be bothered. We know that Chavez has a real concern for us." Angie told me of her plans to join the lettuce boycott and to stay with it until the conflict was settled.

Other field workers told me that they knew nothing about the Teamsters but preferred the Chavez union because it had won in Delano. A few made references to the fast conducted by Cesar and said that he was willing to suffer for the farm workers.

The most effective period of the Salinas strike lasted more than a month from the middle of August until September 22, when the lettuce boycott began. There were bitter confrontations with growers, Teamsters, police, and sheriff's deputies. Cesar conducted marches, demonstrations, and went on a personal fast for nonviolence. The town of Salinas became bitterly polarized. Because UFWOC supporters carried the red flag with the black Aztec eagle, the opposition, consisting of growers, Teamsters, and ranch foremen, adopted the American flag as their symbol. Letters to the editor at the local newspaper protested the latter use of the American flag as a rallying symbol against the predominantly Mexican and Mexican-American constituency of the Chavez group. Racism showed its ugly face on several occasions. A "citizens committee" with vigilante overtones was formed, and serious violence was averted because of pressure from outside church groups, labor leaders, and the cautious cooperation of local law-enforcement agencies. Cesar saw a vicious pattern forming, with deep roots in California's turbulent past farm-labor disputes. He sent a telegram to the state attorney general, who sent two investigators to survey the situation.

The toughest battles in the strike were fought in the

Salinas Valley, located in Monterey County, referred to as the Salad Bowl of the United States.

The arrival of large, publicly owned conglomerates in the valley in recent years set the scene for one of the bitterest and hardest fought farm-labor conflicts in the history of California agriculture. It was the first time that a farm-labor union had won several contracts negotiated solely on the basis of a strike in the field. In the past, strikes had been broken before they were able to bring growers to the bargaining table. An international boycott had been necessary to bring the grape growers to terms. In Salinas, farm workers were strongly united. Few became strike-breakers. Growers found it difficult to recruit strike-breakers from other areas. Fields remained empty, and vegetable shipments were cut to a third. Workers showed me lettuce fields that had to be plowed under for lack of harvest hands. I also saw fields of cauliflower that had literally gone to seed for lack of harvesters.

The largest growers in the valley are Freshpict, a subsidiary of the Purex Corporation, Chiquita Brands, and Interharvest, the distributing and production subsidiaries of the United Fruit Company. Together with the Bud Antle Farms, these companies control 20 per cent of the lettuce shipped in the United States. Freshpict now controls 42,000 acres of land in California, Arizona, New Mexico, Colorado, and Mexico. The United Fruit Company farms 22,000 acres of land in the Salinas and Imperial valleys and in the Yuma and Phoenix areas of Arizona. Needless to say, the conglomerate size of the farms provides a number of political and economic "handles" for boycott pressure. The old adage holds true: "The bigger they are, the harder they fall."*

---

* According to the *Citrus and Vegetable Magazine,* several other conglomerates have found fertile ground throughout the United States. In Florida, the Ogden Corporation, Gulf-Western, Trans-National Communications, and the Academic Development Corporation have entered the agricultural scene by purchasing farms. The control that these large firms exert over the market has threatened the existence of smaller commercial farms and precipitated investigations by the Federal Trade Commission.

Monterey County produces a vegetable crop worth more than $140 million annually. The principal cash crop of the county is lettuce. In 1969, the valley produced more than $49 million worth of lettuce from 58,000 acres of land. Each year, 30,000 boxcars of lettuce are shipped from the Salinas Valley.

On August 12, UFWOC and the Teamsters reached an agreement mediated by the Catholic Bishops Farm Labor Committee, represented by Monsignor George Higgins. The Teamsters agreed to rescind their contracts with the growers. But Herb Fleming, the president of the Vegetable Growers and Shippers Association, stated on August 21, "We have negotiated proper and legal contracts with the Teamsters Union. They have assured us that they will honor these contracts, and we intend to do the same."

The strike began on August 24. Cesar announced to an outdoor rally of more than 5,000 workers that the good faith of the farm workers had been met with a slap in the face. The workers voted unanimously to walk out of the fields after a lengthy moratorium had been granted to the growers.

Two days after the strike began, Jerry Cohen and Venustiano Olguin, an UFWOC organizer, were attacked by a Teamster organizer named Tiny at the Hansen ranch near Salinas. Tiny, who weighed some 290 pounds, put Cohen into the hospital with a concussion. Meanwhile, William Grami, director of organization for the Western Conference of Teamsters denounced the strike as a violation of the August 21 "nonaggression pact." The frequent acts of violence by Teamsters and grower agents were in direct proportion to the effectiveness of the strike. Strawberry shipments had been cut from 13,045 crates to 1,788 crates in two days. Lettuce shipments had been cut to one third, and prices began to rise at retail outlets.

Local courts immediately began issuing antipicketing injunctions, and the city of Salinas even passed an ordinance against conducting religious services at the farm workers' headquarters. When strikers' chaplain, Father Dave Duran, held three Masses in spite of the ordinance, he was handed three citations by police officers. Jim Drake, of the Migrant Ministry, jokingly told his friends that *God* had just been cited by the Salinas Police Department!

The enthusiasm of the workers was demonstrated each evening at the strike meetings held at UFWOC headquarters. The front of the building was plastered with posters skillfully executed by Andy Zermeno. They showed farm workers clustered near a cross with the caption *No Violencia* (Nonviolence). The workers packed the hall and shouted *Viva la Huelga!* whenever a minor victory was announced. The scene resembled a political convention. Each committee representative carried a sign denoting his ranch—Pic n' Pac, The Garin Company, Interharvest, Oshita Farms, and so on.

During the rallies, the spokesmen for each ranch gave eloquent speeches. I will never forget the oration delivered by Antonio Sagredo, a lettuce worker from Gonzales. "Let the people and government of the United States know that we are ready to work," he said. "But let them know that we must have what we ask for. It isn't very much. We don't ask the impossible, only that they look upon us as human beings. We have the same ambitions as they do. We have families and rights. We are people. Why must they continue to treat us like beasts of burden and look for a thousand ways to keep us down? They sold us out to the Teamsters, and now they are angry at us for not selling out. They would lose their crops rather than give in. But the people know that we are right. They will give us their support. We shall triumph!"

"The committees at each ranch were furious at the Teamsters," Father Duran told me. "The workers had been told to sign the Teamster authorization cards or be fired. They refused to sign. There were several spontaneous walkouts by workers all over the area before the big strike started. There was a lot of pent-up resentment when the pot finally boiled over. We had to constantly remind the workers about our pledge of nonviolence. A few of them had begun to throw rocks at the labor contractors' buses."

The strikers assembled at 4 A.M. each morning at the union office then proceeded to the fields in a car caravan. Clusters of pickets with their red union flags could be seen along Highway 101 from Gilroy, north of Salinas, to King City, more than fifty miles to the south.

Violent confrontations continued. An irate foreman plowed into strikers' cars near a farm, doing heavy damage to the vehicles. Pickets were injured when a tractor driver drove his pulverizer near the picket line, showering the pickets with dirt and rocks. Sheriff's deputies intervened, only when their own vehicles were in danger.

At the height of the strike, heavy financial losses and the threat of an international boycott of the United Fruit Company caused Interharvest to rescind its contract with the Teamsters and sign a contract with UFWOC. The benefits of the Teamsters' pact paled into insignificance when compared with the new UFWOC agreement. Field hands received a minimum wage of $2.10 an hour as opposed to the Teamsters' $1.85 "sweetheart" agreement. The Teamster accord increased only to $1.96 at the end of four years. The UFWOC agreement was for two years, to be increased to $2.15 at the end of the second year. It included a ban on such dangerous pesticides as Aldrin, DDT, and DDD, one week's paid vacation, a hiring hall, the Kennedy Health Plan, and a demand to end the profiteering on food and rent at labor camps. The contract was negotiated with the help of a committee elected by the workers.

Growers, Teamsters, and local bigots immediately began to picket the warehouses of Interharvest, distributing bumper stickers that read, "Boycott La Chiquita Bananas," and "Reds, Lettuce Alone!" The newly formed Citizens for Local Justice were angry with the Bishops

Committee and issued their own bumper sticker that said, "Boycott the Church, Pray Direct!" The group held an anti-Chavez rally, complete with hundreds of American flags, martial music, and picket signs proclaiming "Grower Power" and "Support Your Local Grower." Shipping operations at Interharvest were shut down for several days but began again when local police dispersed citizens who had been blocking entrances.

As the strike continued, other growers agreed to recognize UFWOC: among them, Freshpict and D'Arrigo Brothers. When the sheriff's department attempted to enforce antipicketing injunctions against UFWOC on September 13, Cesar led several women pickets in a procession, openly defying the injunction. Deputies declined to arrest the group, claiming that Chavez was "using" the department. But Cesar responded "We welcome arrests. We will not resist. We will conduct ourselves peacefully. We feel that, if we give up the right to picket lines, we give up the right to be a union."

When Judge Anthony Brazil, of Monterey County, forbade further picketing and upheld the validity of the Teamster "sweetheart" contracts, Cesar announced a nationwide boycott of lettuce.

One of the final events of the lettuce strike was a celebration of the Mass held near the Southern Pacific Railroad tracks near Chualar, south of Salinas. More than 3,000 workers gathered for a memorial service honoring thirty-one Mexican farm workers who had been killed seven years previously when the flimsy truck they were traveling in collided with a train. It was one of the many accidents that occurred because of the callous disregard of growers toward their workers. During the Mass, at the time when the dead are remembered, farm workers from the home states of the deceased solemnly read their names over the loudspeaker.

A cold wind blew across the Salinas Valley floor as the strikers returned to their homes in Soledad, Chualar,

Greenfield, Salinas, and Hollister. On the other side of the western mountains, the Monterey Jazz Festival was about to begin. But the lettuce strikers looked to the east because, within a week, many of them would be traveling to cities throughout the United States to tell the American public about their plight. They would ask them to support their boycott, which held the key to a better future for farm workers throughout California and the nation.

[17]

Agbayani:
A Village
with a Future

On July 27, 1970, most of the twenty-five Delano grape growers sat at the collective-bargaining table across from the farm workers' negotiating team, headed by Dolores Huerta and attorney Jerry Cohen.

One of the highlights of the final bargaining session was an unexpected and very moving speech from a man who had remained silent during most of the proceedings. He represented our side. His name is Phillip Veracruz, one of the vice-presidents. He had joined the strike, like many other elderly and unmarried Filipinos, in the very beginning of the dispute.

The subject matter was the many labor camps that house Filipino workers in the grape-growing areas east of Delano. The growers claimed they needed to deduct

ten cents an hour while the men were working to keep
the camps in operation. If the union did not allow this
deduction, they added, they would probably be forced to
close the camps. One of the corporation growers made an
emotional appeal for the deduction, claiming that the
farming business was not as profitable as it used to be.
Closing the camps would indeed be tragic, he stated, but
it might become an economic necessity.

Phillip Veracruz rose from his seat. In a well-measured
voice, he began to speak. He pointed to the blond-haired
son of one of the growers. "I remember when he was a
very small boy," Phillip said, brushing his own gray hair
back with his right hand. "I worked for his father. This
boy used to play out in the vineyards when we were at
work. I saw his father's business expand, year after year,
until today. He is now one of the most prosperous growers
in the area. It would indeed be inhumane to throw these
men out of the camps now—after they have contributed so
many years and so much sweat to produce this wealth for
you."

The growers' eyes were riveted on Phillip. They knew
what he was talking about. They understood his sincerity.
And they were undoubtedly embarrassed by the revelation
he made before the entire group.

"So don't tell me how rough things are, gentlemen. You
claim you have good years and bad years. You chide yourselves for overexpending when you have a good season. I
want to tell you that you have a lot to show for your hard
work. But what do the Filipinos have?" Phillip's voice
shook with emotion as he slowly and deliberately finished
his last sentence. "All we have to show for all our years
of toil are the shirts on our backs."

Phillip sat down and the growers shifted nervously in
their seats. Dolores Huerta continued the discussion on
the camps. It would be a matter, added attorney John
Giumarra, Jr., that would have to be worked out to the
mutual satisfaction of both the growers and the workers.

Andy Imutan, a Filipino vice-president of UFWOC told me of his concern about his Filipino brothers in the labor camps. "Over 30,000 Filipinos came to California to work on the farms over the past forty years," he told me. "Over 90 per cent of them are now over sixty years of age. We must work fast to build them retirement centers. It's the least we can do to return them the dignity they lost when they came to this country. And this is *their* country. They left the Philippines as young men. They have no intention of returning there."

"For five years, I have worked to build this union," Andy said emphatically. "But now I want to do something just for the Filipinos. I really carried those guys in my heart when I worked on the boycott in Baltimore, Washington, D.C., and New York. But now there is not a waking moment of the day when I do not think of those men. They're not only in the camps in Delano and in Coachella, but in the Imperial Valley, in Arizona, and in many other parts of California, such as Stockton and Salinas." The young Filipino organizer is not alone in his concern for the Filipinos. Assistant director Larry Itliong has also voiced concern for the Filipinos, a long-neglected minority in the agricultural work force.

In 1943, Carey McWilliams devoted a chapter of his book *Brothers Under the Skin* to the problems of Filipino immigrants in the United States. He spoke of the exploitation of Filipino farm workers in California. He spoke of the lack of security these men would experience when they grew old. "They will soon find themselves physically incapable of carrying on the strenuous types of field work in which they are now engaged. What will happen, therefore, ten, fifteen or twenty years from now, when most of these 'boys' will be fifty and sixty years old?" McWilliams underestimated the stamina of these men. Many seventy and older are still active in the vineyards and the asparagus and lettuce fields of California. Many of them have died standing up, giving their last gasp of breath to an agricultural system that has had little regard for them as human beings.

It is still a common practice for these men to be expelled from farm labor camps where they have lived for years, merely because they are no longer an economic asset to a grower. If they become old and sickly, they are told that they are in a labor camp and not in a hospital. In most cases, they have nowhere to go. What meager savings they have are swallowed up in high rents.

During the 1930's, some 35,000 Filipinos immigrated to the United States. Of that number, 93 per cent were males, and 7 per cent were females. About 75 per cent of the Filipinos who came to California were single. To make matters worse, five western states, including California, had laws forbidding marriage between Caucasians and non-Caucasians. Such was the ruling of the California Civil Code, which was passed in 1884 and not revoked until the late 1940's.

The Filipinos came because there was a need for a large number of docile, underpaid, and unorganized workers, especially in agriculture. So the steamship lines, eager for passenger profits, cooperated with farm employers and U.S. business interests and did a high-pressure publicity campaign to attract young Filipinos. Great promises were made to them about future opportunities in America. But all they found was exploitation and racism. While their own brothers were defending U.S. interests in the bloody campaigns of World War II, lobbyists in Congress were seeking to exclude and deport Filipinos from the United States.

Filipino immigrants encountered racial prejudice and discrimination wherever they went. The very California growers who brought them to the farms perpetuated anti-Filipino feelings. Dr. George Clements of the Los Angeles Chamber of Commerce called them "the most worthless, unscrupulous, shiftless, diseased semi-barbarians that ever came to our shores." Anti-Filipino riots broke out in the states of California and Washington in 1930 because of such bigotry. Whites were often suspicious and jealous of

Filipinos seen in the company of white women. Whites also claimed that Filipino immigration was responsible for the loss of their own jobs in factories as well as on the farms. This claim, like the others, has never been proven. It seems that the Filipino, like other minority groups, has become the scapegoat for all the ills of society.

Agbayani Village is named in honor of Paulo Agbayani, a Filipino farm worker who died of a heart attack while working as a picket. The idea of a retirement village took shape during a series of meetings conducted by Filipino farm workers in 1968–69. Their aim in establishing the village was to provide a center where single men can live communally after they have completed their work in the fields and vineyards.

"The men don't want the traditional kind of retirement home," Phillip Veracruz said. "Those places are too confining. The men want a place where they can have some freedom. They like to garden. They also want to enjoy their own Filipino culture."

"We are looking forward to the time when we can have a place of our own," George Ebale told me. Ebale, a sixty-nine-year-old striker, was expelled from a labor camp when he went on strike in 1965. "All we had to eat for three months was boiled cabbage and rice. We have been through some rough times. It would be wonderful to have a place to live when we get old.

"We need a place with nurses and doctors. We also need a tract of land, where the men can raise crops and animals. We would like to establish a service center so that we can contact the families of the workers who are still in the Philippines. Too often these men become ill and die. Nobody knows anything about it."

Agbayani Village will hopefully close a sad chapter of California history—the inhumane treatment of the Filipino farm worker. It promises him a place to live in dignity and harmony with his fellow workers. This promise was made, but never kept, by the industry that has enslaved him for so many years—California agriculture.

[18]

The Aftermath

After the historic contracts had been concluded in Delano, thousands of farm workers converged at Forty Acres in order to sign with the union. All available union personnel were assigned to the vineyards to explain the new contracts and answer the questions of the workers.

A factor that complicated the arrival of the union was the short harvest season of 1970. Growers had decreased their table-grape production, anticipating another year of the boycott. The result was the shortest harvest season in fifteen years. Many workers had to be laid off. Many others had arrived in Delano from all parts of the Southwest. They thought that, because the strike was over, there would be abundant work for everyone.

The workers welcomed us when we went to the vineyards. Several apologized for not having left the area during the strike: they supported us, they said, but had to support their families too.

An immense task still lay ahead for UFWOC's organizers in the vineyards from Fresno to Bakersfield. Contracts had been signed, but there was the problem of enforcement. This meant constant vigilance. Strong ranch committees were needed at each farm—people who would stand up for the rights of their fellow workers. Several growers immediately began to cut corners on the contracts. Crew bosses and contractors who had always been antiunion were still seeking ways to fight the union. They felt that it was only a matter of time before they lost their positions of privilege with the growers. They proved to be right.

Over 10,000 workers and hundreds of vineyard crews were covered by the new contracts. Growers and labor contractors were violating the contracts by hiring their own workers without contacting the union. They were also setting piece rates for the picking at variance with union standards.

Five organizers were placed in charge of enforcing the contracts. One of them was Pete Velasco, who had been with the strike since its inception and had been active in the Coachella Valley strike. I accompanied Pete and another Filipino organizer, Apolonio Benson, in a visit to several ranches.

"Martin Zaninovich has been the most cooperative, so far," Pete told me. "I can't say the same about some of the others."

Pete told me that he discovered a grower hiring high school students and paying them lower wages in direct violation of the contract. "I told him that he was stabbing us in the back, that I had been honest with him—why couldn't he be honest with me? He looked at me sheepishly," Pete said with a grin, "and promised not to do it again."

We arrived at a vineyard. The pickers, working in a mobile packing shed, greeted us. A truck, heavily laden with boxes of juicy grapes, stood near the vines.

I commented on the good quality of the grapes. "There's a lot of money tied up in those grapes," Pete said. "At the price these grapes are sold, the average worker is making about $20 an hour for the grower. We have worked like mules all these years and have not received anything in return for our labor."

"You worked like hell," Benson spoke up, "and you only made your life a year shorter." He laughed to hide the bitterness, picked a grape from a plump cluster on the vines, and popped it into his mouth.

Pete indulged in friendly chatter with several pickers and truck-loaders at the next ranch. We discussed a tragic occurrence as we walked down the dusty road between the vines. A rancher's son had just died from an overdose of heroin. At Pete's request, I had composed a telegram to the grieving family on behalf of the union. Two workers had sworn that the youth would have never died if the police had done their job. One of them said, "The cops' knew those kids were using the stuff. They shake down the Chicanos every two minutes, but they will never touch a grower's son. All this could have been taken care of long ago. But they let it go too far."

The scene in Salinas gave us all a sense of hope. The workers were militant, enthusiastic, and determined to build a strong union. They were convinced of the power of their brotherhood. They believed, even though some of them failed at times, in the strange and often mystic force of *no violencia*. Everyone was alive and excited and involved. No one was depressed or discouraged. This, to me, was nonviolence at its finest.

The vibrance and charisma of the movement became more apparent to me as I spoke to a young man who had drifted into the strike in Salinas. He was thin, had long hair, and drove a battered Volkswagen convertible. I spoke with him as we headed toward a picket line outside Salinas. "It's really sensational here," he told me. "It's really beautiful, man. This Chavez guy totally turns me on. Like, this is the only place in the country where there's a real belief and feeling for nonviolence. I've been all over the country raising bread for different groups, but you always run into the violence thing. But this is great, man."

A general meeting was called a few days later, on September 15, 1970. The grape boycotters had returned from all over the United States. Their new task was to meet with the lettuce strikers and to show them how to boycott.

We met in the Santa Cruz Mountains near Watsonville, at a place called Greenwood Lodge. One of the most eloquent talks was given by Al Rojas, a Chicano boycott organizer who had spent two years in Pittsburgh. Al's account of his arrival in Pittsburgh was most interesting.

Rojas is short and stocky, with a round, sincere face. Like most of the young Chicano organizers, he dresses simply, sports a mustache, and wears a union button on his jacket.

He explained that a sympathetic priest had made motel accommodations for his family and two strike volunteers. "It was one of those fancy motels in the downtown section of Pittsburgh. It had fifteen stories and a big water fountain near the entrance. When the doorman asked for our luggage, we were really embarrassed. Our belongings were stuffed into paper bags. My wife, Maria Elena, myself, and the kids looked a sorry sight, ragged and tired from our long journey across the country. On one occasion, some very well-dressed people were having a party. When they saw me in the elevator, one of them asked me if I worked in the kitchen! We stayed there two weeks. Our next home was in the black ghetto. Maria Elena had to take the kids to a park once in a while to show them that there really were such things as trees and flowers."

Rojas concluded his talk, reminding future boycotters that they would have to accept the sacrifices and hardships in order to build a powerful base to help their brothers. "This is the only way we are going to pull farm workers out of poverty and ignorance," he said.

The group at Greenwood Lodge was composed of former boycotters, several Anglo volunteers, and the new crop of boycotters from the fields around Salinas. Some of those present had been serving for the past three years as boycott coordinators in various cities throughout the United States. Dale Van Pelt was one of these men. He had graduated from the Pacific School of Religion in Berkeley in 1965. His first assignment had been as a minister in a small town in the San Joaquin Valley.

"It became clear to me," he said, "that farm workers needed job security and better education more than they needed to be good church members." In 1966, Dale and his wife, Jan, joined the movement to build Chavez's union by participating in the strike directly with the workers. In July, 1968, Dale and Jan became boycott organizers in Seattle. They built a consumer organization, made up of housewives, students, ministers, and other volunteers.

Dale felt that the boycott had been a success largely because farm workers had appealed to the good will and decency of the American public. "I'll stay with it as long as they need me," he added. "My hope is that the movement will result in a strong rank-and-file union with a true social conscience."

One of the most promising young leaders to emerge from the boycott was Eliseo Medina. I had worked with the bright twenty-four-year-old farm worker in Chicago for two months. In the three years Eliseo had spent there, he had built a strong organization and literally kept all nonunion grapes out of the city.

Eliseo was born in Zacatecas, Mexico. His father had slipped into California illegally in order to acquire enough money to support his family. When he was ten years old, his mother sold the few skinny livestock they possessed and the family moved to Tijuana to be closer to Eliseo's father. They soon came to Delano and began to work in the nearby vineyards.

Medina became interested in the union after the strike had started. "I read in the Spanish edition of *El Malcriado* that a crooked labor contractor had been caught cheating the people. I knew that Chavez was really out to help us," he said. "Then, one day, my mother came home and shouted with a big smile on her face: *'Estamos en huelga, mi hijo!'* [We're on strike, son!]. Before I knew it, I was involved. Dolores Huerta made me a picket captain one day. She also got me involved in the Di Giorgio election.

"Immediately after the strike started against Giumarra," Eliseo continued, "I was sent to Chicago with the names of five people—three of whom had left the city—a bag of union buttons, and $100."

The Catholic Archdiocese of Chicago had given Eliseo and his fellow volunteers office space in its Office for the Spanish-Speaking on South Wabash Avenue.

"As we organized the boycott, I learned one thing," Eliseo told the assembled volunteers, in his slightly accented English. "It's better to concentrate on the average man in the streets than with the top level people like mayors, congressmen, and other leaders. Many of these people give you their support, but you need a solid base. Our method was to contact every possible group we could find: Jewish groups, Catholic groups, Protestant groups, labor, students, you name it! Sometimes we had as many as forty or fifty meetings a week. We asked people to contribute money. We started a newsletter to keep our contacts informed as to what was happening in California and throughout the country. Our biggest battle was with the Jewel Tea Company, the largest market chain in Chicago. The company was afraid to have its liberal image tarnished, since they had sponsored community projects in the ghetto areas. After a long struggle, Jewel agreed to take the grapes off. The rest of the chains followed suit in rapid order."

The young organizer told me of his hopes for the farm workers' movement. "We have been successful because we haven't withdrawn into a shell. We haven't excluded ourselves from the rest of society. We know that the system doesn't have it in for any particular race or group. It screws all the poor people. That's why all the poor people, all the races, have to unite to change the system. This is what our union stands for. The boycott was successful primarily because a bunch of illiterate farm workers went out across the nation and worked their tails off! They didn't get involved in side issues or movement rhetoric. They just had one goal in mind: to get the grapes off the shelves. And that's what they accomplished!"

Medina summed up his ideas on nonviolence in a few brief sentences. "We just refused to get hung up on hating anyone, because that's not productive," he said. "It's so easy to shoot someone. But what have you accomplished? It's harder to move ahead slowly, with many discouragements. But all this time is spent building a powerful base. The boycott really tore them apart. The only way to make real change is to organize, organize, organize!"

"What about politics?" I asked Eliseo.

"To me there's no real difference between the Democratic and Republican parties as they now stand," he answered. "They are both equally nonrepresentative of the wishes of the poor. In order to have political power, you must have economic power behind you. This is what we are building—economic power. Chicanos have an old saying, you know: *Con el dinero baila el perro* [If you have money, you can even make a dog dance]."

The scene at Greenwood Lodge was symbolic of what the Delano movement could offer the country. Middle-class college students, ministers, priests, housewives, and farm workers clustered together and shared their common experiences. It was like a university seminar devoted to the specific needs of the poor who struggled for self-determination.

Hijinio Rangel had been a boycott organizer in Detroit. He told the group that Cesar had asked him if he were willing to give up what he had to work on the boycott. Hijinio smiled as he related his answer. "I told Cesar that I was disposed to lose everything I had. But I didn't really have much! Since I had two days to prepare my family for the trip, I asked some friends to make some furniture payments for me. At first I wasn't sure I could do the job. But I remembered what Cesar had told me: 'We don't want people who know how to do the job, but don't want to do the job. We want people who may not know what to do, but really want to learn how to do the job.'

"I'll tell you why I joined the movement. I saw the old people, beaten down after so many years of working like animals. I made up my mind that I'm not going to be treated that way all my life. I made up my mind that I'm not going to end up that way. When I met Cesar, I knew that he was the man that could help us."

The list of UFWOC organizers goes on indefinitely. Each has an intensely interesting story that I hope will someday be told.

"These people have undergone some fantastic changes in the last few years," Gil Padilla, a UFWOC vice-president told me. "Nobody is going to push them around anymore. They are going to build the most powerful union in this country. I think that other groups will look to our union and want to learn how we did it. I think the important element is that this union recognizes that everyone has potential. The strike and the boycott brought out this potential. Besides, we had a long-range plan with specific goals. You add dedication to this, and you come up with some very big successes."

As I looked into the crowd, I saw these people: Mac and Diana Lyons from the New York boycott; Ramon Pasillas, who had worked in Kansas City with his family; Alfredo and Juanita Herrera, who had boycotted in Denver; Manuel Vasquez and his brother Mike and wife, Carolina, who had worked in Washington, D.C., and Connecticut. Marcos Muñoz, one of the most effective boycotters in the country, was still in Boston persuading the S. S. Pierce Company to negotiate with UFWOC for its strawberry farms in the Salinas Valley. These were only a few of the leaders responsible for organizing the grape-boycott victory.

Just before we left the lodge, I talked with Ramon Pasillas, a soft-spoken organizer whose father had come to Delano in 1921.

"This movement had to come," he told me. "The worst thing was the way they treated you, man. I remember the time I asked a foreman for a match. He waited until I got up to the truck he was driving, then deliberately dropped the matches on the ground." Ramon looked down in disgust.

"I often thought about things like this when the boycott work became discouraging," he said. "The growers really made us suffer. Now they are going to have to treat us with dignity. That's what it's all about. We're not slaves anymore."

We left the meeting. In our effort, I had shared some tremendously meaningful human encounters. Behind all the facts and figures and beyond all the paper work and contracts, the strike was made up of human beings.

Epilogue:
At the Salinas Jail

"I'm in good spirits, and they're very kind to me. I was spiritually prepared for this confinement; I don't think the judge was unfair. I am prepared to pay the price for civil disobedience. I am still very committed, and I'm not bitter at all.

"At this point in our struggle there is more need than ever to demonstrate our love for those who oppose us. Farm workers are wounded every day by being denied representation of the union of their choice. Jail is a small price to pay to help right that injustice."

—Statement released by Cesar Chavez from
the Monterey County jail, December 5, 1970

Salinas was wet, cold, and windy on the morning of December 4, when Cesar was to appear in court before Monterey County Superior Court Justice Gordon Campbell. Chavez was to show cause why he had not obeyed an earlier court order, which demanded that he terminate the boycott against the lettuce-growing company of Bud Antle Produce.

191

I arrived at the Farm Workers Office on East Alisal Street at 8 A.M. in a drizzling rain. Hundreds of workers were arriving from all over California to join the mass demonstration at the courthouse. I recognized faces from Coachella, Fresno, Fillmore, Delano, Earlimart, Bakersfield, and several other farm towns. A procession was formed, led by the officers of the union: Larry Itliong, Dolores Huerta, Phillip Veracruz, Julio Hernandez, Andy and Luming Imutan, and Gil Padilla. Father Dave Duran asked me to join him near the head of the column, but I decided to drop back and walk with Eloise, one of Cesar's daughters.

We started to sing strike songs as we walked toward the courthouse, some ten blocks away. After we had walked a few blocks, I looked back. The crowd had swelled to well over a thousand. The *huelga* flags and pictures of Our Lady of Guadalupe were everywhere. As we approached downtown Salinas, a man parked his pickup near us and fastened an American flag to his radio antenna. He began shouting and shaking his fists angrily at the marchers.

"What did he say?" I asked Eloise.

She smiled. "He said that Mexico was *that* way!" she said, pointing southward. Just as she finished speaking, a picket captain told the marchers not to answer the taunts. "*Silencio,*" he said, in a serious voice.

Ahead of us marched Elizabeth, Eloise's younger sister, and Suzy Chavez, their cousin. A few minutes later, Cesar joined the march with Manuel Uranday, one of his bodyguards. Manuel's wife, Esther, is a close friend of Helen Chavez. Both women had walked picket lines together since the grape strike began and still spend six days a week in UFWOC's offices.

The march on the Salinas courthouse coincided with reports that the lettuce boycott was successful, despite grower propaganda to the contrary. In two short months of boycotting, sufficient pressure had been applied to induce Freshpict, the Purex subsidiary, to sign a contract with UFWOC. Shortly after the signing, Freshpict's president, Howard Leach, and its northern California manager, Daryl Arnold, both resigned from their posts, calling the agreement "inflationary and unrealistic." It seems odd to me that these affluent agribusiness executives could have pangs of conscience regarding the modest contract gained by the UFWOC bargaining team.*

On the same eventful day, December 4, Pic'N'Pac, the S. S. Pierce subsidiary, signed a contract with UFWOC, and Judge Anthony Brazil issued an injunction banning all boycott activities against Bud Antle Produce. The ruling was that Antle had been under contract with Teamsters Local 890 since 1961.

On October 26, the Teamsters, represented by their acting president Frank Fitzsimmons, and president George Meany, of the AFL-CIO, reached an accord that UFWOC would continue to represent field workers, while the Teamsters would have jurisdiction over workers in food-processing plants, warehouses, and markets.

But the question still remained: What was to be done about the two hundred contracts that the Teamsters had hurriedly signed with lettuce and vegetable growers in four California valleys? Teamster organizer William Grami could only say that the contracts were in a state of limbo and that all dues collected from the workers were being held in escrow.

On November 17, Justice Campbell ordered UFWOC to post a $2.75 million bond in the event that financial damage might accrue to Bud Antle Produce because of the boycott.

As Cesar Chavez entered the Monterey County courthouse, he knew that it would be difficult to fight the con-

* During a subsequent nationally televised debate, Cesar charged that Arnold had walked out because he refused to deal with Mexicans. Arnold replied that he had dealt with Mexicans all his life. "Sure," Cesar responded, "as field hands. But you didn't want to deal with Mexicans in positions of leadership and power."

tempt-of-court charge. Campbell was a longtime friend of some of the Salinas growers, and, as an attorney, had defended the growers in previous labor disputes.

The corridors of the courthouse were jammed with farm workers. A newsman later remarked, "You couldn't hear a sound. You would never know all those people were out there."

Seated in the dock were Cesar Chavez and the attorneys for the defense, Jerry Cohen and William Carder. On the opposite side were two members of the Antle family and their attorneys, Richard B. Maltzman and Philip Bass.

UFWOC's position remained that it was in excess of the court's jurisdiction and unconstitutional to be compelled to obey an order that was under appeal. Bud Antle had refused to negotiate with UFWOC and wanted to continue his "sweetheart" relationship with Teamsters Local 890. UFWOC further asserted that many field workers were never covered by the contract until September, 1970, when Chavez arrived in the valley.

Father Austin Morris, a professor of labor law at the University of San Francisco, had made a study of the Antle contract. "The Teamsters loaned money to Antle in order to bail him out of bankruptcy in the early '60s," Morris told me. "The contract between Antle and the Teamsters was the strangest thing I ever saw. Even though the rest of the growers were furious at Antle for signing it, it was merely a legal formality and literally had no provisions to better the conditions of the workers. To call it a sweetheart contract would be putting it mildly. It seems to me that the contract could have no binding force, either legally or morally, since it was executed with a company-assisted union. The proof of this came when Chavez called the strike. Eighty per cent of Antle's workers walked out on strike, favoring UFWOC. These workers certainly had no allegiance to the Teamsters union."

Since the Dow Chemical Company had purchased

17,000 acres of land from Bud Antle and later leased it back to Antle, a boycott was initiated against Dow. Dow also makes harmful pesticides that for years have injured and maimed farm workers throughout the United States.

Seated in the courtroom were several Chavez supporters, including UFWOC's board of directors. Helen Chavez sat with her sons, Anthony and Paul, and two of her daughters, Ana and Linda. Several priests led more than 2,000 workers in prayer outside the courthouse.

A high point of the hearing was the testimony read by Antle attorney Maltzman. He read a deposition he had earlier taken of Cesar. "I asked Mr. Chavez," he said, " 'Do you mean to tell me that, if Bud Antle signs a contract with UFWOC, your organizers will call off their boycott against Dow Chemical?' "

With the understatement that Cesar often uses in such circumstances, he replied, "Well, I can't say for sure. You know, once the students pick up on a thing like this [a boycott against Dow], you never know what might happen. The students, you know, have always been rather upset about Dow's participation in the war." Cesar added that he had recently visited several eastern university campuses and called upon students to boycott Dow products. "We feel that Dow and Antle are working together on a variety of projects. We are now doing research and gathering information to find out just how extensive this collusion is."

After more than four hours of court proceedings, Campbell found Cesar in contempt of court, fined him $1,000, and sentenced him to jail indefinitely until he "called off the boycott against Bud Antle, Inc., and the Dow Chemical Corporation."

As we left the courtroom, I could see that Helen Chavez, a strong and vivacious woman, was angry. Weeping, Sally Chavez, her sister-in-law, embraced her. A rally was held outside the courthouse and Cesar's request to the

farm workers was announced over a bullhorn and before
the TV cameras: "Boycott Antle! Boycott Dow! Boycott
the Hell Out of Them!"

The farm workers were also angry and shouted *Lo
Compraron!* and *Vamos todos a la carcel!* (They bought
off the judge! and If Cesar goes to jail, we all go!).

Dolores Huerta and Larry Itliong then spoke to the
crowd. Itliong told the workers that this was another example of how the growers can utilize the power of the
courts "to keep us poor." But Dolores and Itliong asked
for a tough but nonviolent effort against Dow and Antle.
"Let us work nonviolently and boycott Dow and Antle
from one end of the world to the other," Dolores said.

A few days later, Ethel Kennedy paid a surprise visit to
Cesar at the Salinas jail. Ethel, wearing a navy-blue pants
suit, was escorted to a candlelight vigil and Mass outside
the jail by Jerry Cohen and Rafer Johnson, the athlete,
who was acting as her bodyguard. Two thousand workers
attended the service. On the opposite side of the street,
three hundred "citizens committee" pickets shouted,
"Ethel, Go Home" and several other epithets directed
against the Kennedy family. Among the opposition were
several "prominent" Salinas growers. Their ugly performance, carried by nationwide television, undoubtedly
gained more supporters for UFWOC's cause.

"They couldn't have done more for us if they had hired
fifty apes," Jerry Cohen told me. "Ethel locked arms with
Rafer Johnson and me. We were surrounded by a cordon
of sheriff's deputies as we entered the jail. Even with all
that protection, some grower tried to hit Ethel or grab
her hair. A deputy threw him a karate chop that caused
him to recoil in pain. After we had arrived in the visitors'
section of the jail, Ethel turned to me and said, 'Gee, you
guys throw weird parties!' With that, the tension broke,
and we all laughed hilariously!"

I thought of Senator Robert F. Kennedy's two previous
visits to Delano and said to Jerry that the Kennedy wit

and presence were always with us when we needed them.

Shortly thereafter, in mid-December, Mrs. Coretta Scott King came to the Salinas jail to show her support for Cesar.

And finally, two days before Christmas, Cesar was released, by order of the California State Supreme Court, pending the hearing of his appeal.

Late in December, I paid visits to three individuals whose views and opinions on the farm-labor struggle I respect.

It was raining in Los Angeles when I visited Sam Kushner, a heavy-set, middle-aged man who is the southern California bureau chief of the *People's World* newspaper. Sam's coverage of *la huelga* has earned him the respect of all those who have engaged in the struggle for social justice in California. Sam, a Jew, learned, from his early years on New York's Lower East Side, the meaning of poverty and persecution. His personal experiences as a labor-union organizer and journalist during the crucial years of trade unionism qualified him to see the Delano struggle from a unique perspective.

Sam never missed an important event in Delano. His Communist Party affiliation made him and the strikers he wrote about the natural targets of red-baiters and John Birchers. Labor leaders had been criticized for even speaking to Sam. He jokingly told me one day, "How do you think my friends feel about my being seen with *them*?"

As we sat in his office, Sam told me about his many visits to Delano. Just before Sam underwent surgery in 1969, someone had asked Cesar to wish Sam good health. "Cesar told me that he would pray for me," Sam said, smiling and puffing on his omnipresent pipe. " 'Fine, Cesar,' I told him. 'You do *your* thing, and I'll do *my* thing!' "

Sam and I talked at length about the strikes in Delano and Salinas. I asked him what he felt was the real significance of the recent victories. "I think that the hiring hall is the best thing that ever happened to farm workers. The fact that a worker still has to work under a labor contractor in many places is one of the most degrading things about agriculture. The hiring hall does away with all the abuses of the labor contractors.

"I will never forget the time I covered the infamous 'shape up' in Calexico. Thousands of farm workers come across the border in the wee hours of the morning from Mexicali in order to find work in the Imperial Valley. Labor contractors choose the most able-bodied workers and load them into trucks and buses. The weak and the aged are left behind.

"On this occasion, I noticed a very young and attractive girl, who appeared to have been left behind. I asked her opinions about the labor contractors and growers. Much to my surprise, she had nothing but praise for them. I asked some other workers standing nearby why this girl had so much love for the bosses. They laughed. 'Well, because she sleeps with the foremen,' one of them said. 'That's why she can get any job she wants. She just didn't feel like working today.'

"So you see," Sam continued, "under the hiring hall system, the worker does not have to sell himself. There is fairness and justice for all. A sense of dignity for the worker is always the most important gain in a struggle like this."

After I spoke to Sam, I drove north to Santa Maria. The strikers there had asked me to say a Mass for Cesar, who was still in the Salinas County jail. Over two hundred workers attended the service. When I told them what had happened to Ethel Kennedy at the Salinas jail, I could hear them gasp with horror and disgust. During the Mass, I emphasized the importance of Cesar's sacrifice in jail. I said that the growers in Santa Maria and Salinas would soon agree to negotiate with UFWOC. "But Cesar did not go to jail merely to get contracts and pay increases," I told them. "He wants to bring about changes in our society so that people will respect one another—so that men like Reagan and Agnew will find themselves out of office. If we stay united and dedicated to helping our brothers, then we can change this society. It will never be changed by money or by violence. It can only be changed for the better by nonviolent action and the spiritual power it generates."

After the Mass, the workers wrote notes to Cesar and asked me to take them to the jail in Salinas. One of the workers gave me a box of freshly picked artichokes to give to Helen Chavez and the people in Delano.

When I arrived back in Delano, I spoke to Richard and Sally Chavez. Richard told me that Freddie, his son, had been sentenced to a weekend in jail for his part in the high school disturbance described in Chapter 12. The situation between the youths and the Delano police had become bitterly polarized since the incident. A tragic event had taken place during the summer. Two of the striking students had become involved in a shoot-out with the police. The Western Auto Store, where the boys had been trapped by the police, burned down. One of the boys was being held indefinitely in the juvenile hall. Richard looked depressed as we discussed the situation. "We lost this round," he said. "But the fight is not over with yet."

Two days later, a Basque priest, Father José Ellacuria, a Jesuit, accompanied me on a trip from Delano to Salinas. José, a slightly built man in his forties, had spent five weeks working in UFWOC's offices in Delano. He had familiarized himself with the workings of the union and the philosophy of Chavez. His plans were to develop some union leaders among Formosa's 34 million inhabitants. José had been in Taiwan for fourteen years.

As we drove through the long stretches of the San Joaquin Valley along Highway 99, we discussed the condition of the farm workers. José asked me about the federal subsidies given to the farmers. I explained that President

Nixon had finally signed a bill into law limiting the amount of subsidies available to each farmer to $55,000. "The subsidies will eventually be eliminated," I added, "but there will still be many problems to tackle in the future." I told him that thousands of small farmers were being forced off the land because of the cost-price squeeze and competition from the corporation farms. There would have to be a great deal of planning to prepare for the future. Demographers estimate that 100 million more people would be living in the United States in the next century. The population would have to shift from the cities to the rural areas. I said that our country's public policy would have to be radically altered to improve the quality of life for farm workers whose jobs would be taken away by automation.

José spoke of the problems in his native Spain and expressed anger at the repressive treatment his Basque countrymen had received at the hands of Franco.

In Salinas, the sheriff would not permit us to visit Cesar. That evening, we joined Father Reynaldo Flores, a fellow Franciscan, and celebrated Mass in front of the jail. The workers had set up an altar on the back of a pickup, adorned with a cross, a painting of Our Lady of Guadalupe, and pictures of John and Robert Kennedy. They had been maintaining a continuous vigil since Cesar had been jailed.

After the Mass, José read a telegram sent to Cesar by Bishop Sergeo Mendez Arceo, the famous maverick and progressive Catholic bishop of Cuernavaca, Mexico. He expressed hopes that Cesar would continue his "humanizing efforts" on behalf of farm workers. UFWOC organizer Marshall Ganz told the assembled workers that Harvard University had publicly stated its support of the lettuce boycott and *The New York Times* had expressed its support in a strong editorial. The workers applauded the news. Marshall also announced that the first Mexican-American bishop, Patrick Flores, of San Antonio, Texas, was on his way to pay a visit to Cesar.

José and I stayed at a Franciscan retreat house at nearby San Juan Bautista that evening. Cesar and Helen had spent two weeks there in September, 1970, when Cesar was recovering from the effects of his second major fast. Since that time, the local growers had boycotted the retreat house and harassed the friars who reside there. But the fathers took everything in good spirits and looked forward to the time when they could again offer their hospitality to Cesar and his family.

On the following day, José and I paid a visit to an old friend, Ralph Guzman, a professor of Chicano studies at the University of California at Santa Cruz. The campus is nestled in the hills just above the blue Pacific Ocean. Ralph, dark complexioned, in his forties, and rather heavyset, with a round face and horn-rimmed glasses, greeted us enthusiastically and introduced us to his fellow instructors and to several Chicano students.

Ralph spoke enthusiastically of both the Chicano movement and Cesar's success with the farm workers. I asked him what the Chicanos in the cities thought of Cesar's movement.

"The militant Chicano leaders, like Denver's Corky Gonzales, have a great deal of respect for Cesar," Ralph said. "But very few Chicanos in the barrios are really acquainted with Cesar's ideas and techniques. For one thing, you must realize that life in the barrio street-corner society is violent. Things are very rough in the El Hoyo and Hazard districts of Los Angeles, for example. The people have to be tough to survive. The police, of course, are the most violent of all.

"So you see," Ralph continued, "if somebody starts theorizing about nonviolence, he just might be considered not very manly; *no muy macho*—in the language of the barrio.

"Who knows how successful Cesar could be, if he began to organize in the cities?" he added. "Things are so divided there, and there is so much rhetoric, so many shibboleths, yet very little organization. For years, many institutions have struggled for the minds of our people. The church, the Communist Party, the right wing, the government have all tried to influence our people. Maybe someone like Cesar could unite all the various segments of the Chicano community. One thing is certain—it would be one hell of a job."

Late that afternoon, I dropped José off at the University of San Francisco. He was to depart for Taiwan in two days. Luckily, I was able to contact Fred Ross, who now resides in San Francisco. Fred and his wife, Frances, live in a modest home in the hills above the Mission district. One can see the entire panorama of the city from their bay window.

Ross is a tall and lean man who looks younger than his years. The veteran organizer leaves his hilltop home occasionally to aid Cesar during tough organizing campaigns. I had seen him many times during my stay in Delano and recently in Salinas. At present, he is working on a book dealing with his experiences as an organizer.

Fred concurred with me that the Salinas strike was probably the most successful field workers' strike in the history of U.S. agriculture. I asked him what direction he thought Cesar's movement would take.

"Organizing farm workers has been a very unpredictable situation," Fred stated. "The Delano strike began two or three years ahead of schedule. The Salinas strike was completely unplanned. The growers really set us up for that one."

Fred felt that Cesar's real task was to educate and politicize the farm workers. Many of them need citizenship, so that their voting power can have an effect on local and national politics.

"Many people regard you as the mastermind behind the whole movement, Fred," I said. Before I had finished the sentence, Ross answered with a firm "No, that's not true."

"Cesar received a few ideas and concepts from Alinsky and me," he said. "But he developed his own philosophy and his organizing style. You know how well it has worked."

I asked about the difference between the styles of Alinsky and Chavez. "I think that the major difference is that Cesar has always been committed to the poor and always will be committed to the poor," he answered, in a serious tone. "Alinsky is now concentrating on the middle class. Besides that, Saul's technique as an organizer is to work with existing organizations in a community. Cesar's method has been to organize one person at a time. He has literally built his movement up from the foundations. He has worked like a bricklayer, carefully setting each brick in place."

"But what about the future of the movement?" I asked. "Many people say it will just become like any other union, that it will lose its family spirit and idealism."

"I don't agree with that point of view," Ross rejoined. "Cesar has injected his philosophy of mutual support and cooperation into his whole organization. From the very beginning, Cesar has educated the farm workers as to the significance of cooperatives and credit unions. He has made the farm workers aware of other groups and their problems, too."

I agreed with Fred that Cesar had placed the service-center aspects of his movement on an equal plane with his organizing drives. I recalled entire weeks during the winter months when Cesar had pondered ways to help the needy and even the nonfarm workers in the valley. He had already begun a special experimental school for children of farm workers, called the *Huelga* school. He had discussed plans to expand medical services through the farm workers' clinic. He had purchased a former TB sanatorium near Tehachapi and named it La Paz. La Paz is now UFWOC's cultural and nonviolent-training center. He had spoken to me enthusiastically about purchasing land for the Agbayani Village and about many other cooperative ventures for the poor of the valley.

Fred paused for a moment, as I prepared to leave. Then he smiled and said, "I used to tell Cesar to get his mind off Forty Acres and all those projects. But he insisted on developing his cooperative schemes, even if it meant diminishing his organizing efforts."

In my car, I turned on the radio. The news was typical —the latest gruesome details of the Tate–La Bianca murder trial and the My Lai massacre. As the newscaster began to relate Governor Ronald Reagan's most recent ravings about the high cost, of welfare and medical care for the aged, I switched off the radio. My mind was elsewhere. I was thinking of Cesar, who was still in jail, of Forty Acres, and of dreams that were slowly coming true for thousands of farm workers. I thought of the farm workers in Coachella, Delano, and Salinas and the rallying cries I had shared with them so often:

Que Viva la Huelga!
Que Viva Cesar Chavez!
Que Viva la Causa!

Appendix

The following is a copy of the first major contract signed with the grape industry: the Coachella Valley contract with the David Freedman Company. It set the pattern for all subsequent agreements.

COLLECTIVE BARGAINING AGREEMENT

THIS AGREEMENT is made and entered into at Los Angeles, California as of the 31st day of March, 1970, by and between the party whose name appears on the signature page hereof under the designation of "Company" ("Company" herein) and UNITED FARM WORKERS ORGANIZING COMMITTEE, AFL-CIO (herein "Union").

The parties agree as follows:

SECTION I. *RECOGNITION.*

A. Company does hereby recognize Union as the sole labor organization representing Company's agricultural employees (herein called "workers") and recognizes and agrees to treat and negotiate with Union as the sole and exclusive bargaining agent for and on behalf of such workers on properties owned or leased by Company, and all other workers employed by Company. The term "worker" shall not include supervisory employees with the authority to hire or fire (herein called "Supervisors").

B. Company further recognizes the rights and obligations of Union to negotiate wages, hours and conditions of employment and to administer this Agreement on behalf of all covered employees.

C. Neither Company nor its representatives will take any action to disparage, denigrate or subvert Union, nor will they promote or finance any competing labor organization.

D. Neither Company nor its representatives will interfere with the right of any worker to join and assist Union. Company will make known to all workers that they will secure no advantage, nor more favorable consideration nor any form of special privilege because of non-participation in Union activities.

E. Company will make known to all workers, supervisors, and officers, its policies and commitments as set forth above with respect to recognition of Union and will encourage employees in the bargaining unit to give utmost consideration to supporting and participating in collective bargaining and contract administration functions.

F. Supervisors and other workers not covered by this Agreement shall not perform work on operations performed by workers in the bargaining unit as defined in this Agreement, except for improvement of processes, testing of equipment, and training. Company agrees that this paragraph shall not be used as a basis for the purpose of avoiding the recall of bargaining unit workers from layoff or displacing bargaining unit workers from work they would normally perform.

G. Any claim by Union that on-the-job conduct of any non-bargaining unit employee is disrupting harmonious working relations may be treated as a grievance under the grievance procedures of this contract.

H. There shall be no sub-contracting without prior consultation and agreement with the Union.

SECTION II. *UNION SECURITY*.

A. Union membership shall be a condition of employment. Each worker shall be required to become a member of Union immediately following seven (7) continual calendar days of employment, and to remain a member of Union in good standing. Union shall be the sole judge of the good standing of its members. Any worker who fails to become a member of Union within the time limit set forth herein, or who fails to pay the required initiation fees, periodic dues or regularly authorized assessments as prescribed by Union shall be immediately discharged upon written notice from Union to Company. The preceding sentence is not intended to limit the grounds for determination of good standing.

B. Company agrees to furnish Union, in writing, a list of workers giving the names, addresses, ages, Social Security numbers and type of job classifications.

C. Company agrees to deduct from each worker's pay all initiation fees, periodic dues and assessments as required by Union, upon presentation of individual authorizations, signed by workers, directing Company to make such deductions. Company shall make such deductions from the worker's pay once monthly and shall remit same to Union not later than the 15th day of the following month. Vacation pay is subject to monthly dues deduction. Union will furnish the forms to be used for authorization. Company will furnish Union with a duplicate copy of all signed authorizations.

D. Union shall indemnify and hold Company harmless from and against any and all claims, demands, suits, or other forms of liability that may arise out of or by reason of action taken by Company for the purpose of compliance with any of the provisions of this section.

SECTION III. *SUCCESSOR CLAUSE*.

A. This Agreement shall be binding upon the successors, administrators, executors, and assigns of the parties hereto.

B. In the event a farming operation or part thereof is sold, leased, transferred, conveyed in any manner, or taken over by sale, transfer, assignment, receivership or bankruptcy; such operation shall continue to be subject to the terms and conditions of this Agreement for the life hereof. Company shall give notice of the existence of this Agreement to any purchaser, transferee, lessee, or assignee of the operation covered by this Agreement or any part thereof. Such notice shall be in writing, with a copy to the Union, at the time the seller, transferor, or lessor executes a contract or transaction as herein described.

SECTION IV. *HIRING.*

A. Whenever Company requires workers to perform any work covered by this Agreement, it shall notify Union, stating the number of workers needed, the type of work to be performed, the estimated starting date of the work and the approximate duration thereof. Said preliminary notice shall be given at least two weeks prior to the estimated starting date. Company shall give Union a further notice fixing the exact starting date at least forty-eight hours prior to the date fixed for actual commencement of the work.

B. Upon receipt of said latter notice, Union shall use its best efforts to furnish the requested number of workers. If Union does not furnish the requested number of workers on the date of the beginning of the work, Company shall be free to procure needed workers not furnished by Union from any other source. If Company procures workers from any other source, it will make available to Union, in writing within seven (7) days thereafter, the names, Social Security numbers, job classifications, and addresses of all workers so hired, provided, however, that Union shall be entitled, acting on its own, to ascertain such information from such workers at any time after twenty-four hours following the hiring of such workers. Such workers shall be subject to the provisions of Section II of this Agreement.

C. The number of workers requested by Company shall be

reasonably related to the amount of work to be performed in ratios related to Company's previous practices.

D. Company will notify Union in advance of lay-offs either within seven (7) days, or as quickly as possible, and will furnish Union with a list of those workers that have been laid off either within twenty-four hours or as quickly as reasonably possible thereafter.

E. When filling vacancies and making promotions, demotions, transfers, layoffs, recalls from layoff or reclassification, preference will be given to workers with the greatest seniority provided they have the qualifications to perform the work under normal supervision with reasonable efficiency.

F. Seniority will be defined as the total length of continuous service or actual days worked. Any authorized leave of absence or vacation will be deemed days worked if such time would have been work days. Seniority will not be accumulated during time not worked.

G. If less than the usual work opportunity is available, preference in hiring shall be given to workers with the longest seniority.

H. Union will assume responsibility for compliance with seniority. Company shall be entitled to rely on seniority determinations made by Union, and Union will indemnify Company and hold it harmless of and from any claims, demands, disputes or actions arising out of or in connection with such determinations as shall have been made by Union.

SECTION V. *DISCRIMINATION.*

In accord with policies of Company and Union, it is agreed that neither party will discriminate against any worker on the basis of race, age, creed, color, religion, sex, political belief, national origin, or language spoken.

SECTION VI. *MAINTENANCE OF STANDARDS.*

Company agrees that all conditions of employment for workers relating to wages, hours of work and general working conditions shall be maintained at no less than the highest standards in effect as of the date of this Agreement. Conditions of employment shall be improved wherever specific provisions for improvement are made elsewhere in this Agreement.

SECTION VII. *REPORTING AND STANDBY TIME.*

A. A worker paid on an hourly or piecework basis who is required to report for work and does report and is furnished no work or less than four hours of work for reasons other than Acts of God shall be paid at least four hours for that day at the worker's hourly rate of pay or the worker's average hourly piece rate earnings. The term "Acts of God" shall include, but not be limited to, a drop in allowable sugar content of any particular variety of grape during the first week of harvest only.

B. A worker shall be paid for all time he is required to remain on the job ("standby time") at his hourly rate or average hourly piece rate earnings.

SECTION VIII. *CAMP HOUSING.*

A. Allocation of available camp housing shall be on a non-discriminatory basis without favoritism. The factors of race, color, creed, religion, age, political belief, national origin or language spoken shall not be considered in distribution of available dwellings.

B. Camp housing shall be free of charge. Board shall be operated on a non-profit basis.

SECTION IX. *WORKER SECURITY.*

A. Company agrees that any worker may refuse to pass through any picket line sanctioned by Union.

B. No worker under this Agreement shall be required to perform work that normally would have been done by employees of another Company who are engaged in a strike, or to work on goods that will be handled or are destined to be handled by other workers engaged in strikebreaking.

SECTION X. *CREDIT UNION WITHHOLDING.*

Upon proper written authorization from a worker, deductions as provided for in such authorization shall be made by Company for the Farm Workers Credit Union, and such monies forwarded to that organization.

SECTION XI. *LEAVES OF ABSENCE.*

A leave of absence without pay shall be granted to a worker for a reasonable period for any of the following reasons, without loss of seniority:

A. For jury duty or witness duty;

B. Up to two (2) years for illness or injury of worker requiring absence from the job;

C. A worker of Company who serves his country pursuant to the Selective Service Act shall not lose any seniority, job rights, or other benefit. Upon return from such service, such worker shall be granted a job equal to that he would have had with Company had he remained in Company's continued employ.

D. For valid personal reasons.

SECTION XII. *DISCHARGE.*

A. Company shall have the sole right to discipline and discharge workers for just cause provided that in the exercise of this right it will not act in violation of the terms of this Agreement.

B. Prior to any discharge, Company shall notify a steward and/or Union official and such Union representative shall be present when formal charges are made.

C. The Union representative shall have the right to interview employees in private.

D. Within twenty-four (24) hours after any discharge for

just cause the Union representative will be notified in writing of the reasons for such discharge.

E. Individual performance in relation to a piece rate or incentive plan shall not be conclusive evidence for the purpose of discharging a worker.

SECTION XIII. *LEAVE OF ABSENCE FOR UNION BUSINESS.*

A. Any worker elected or appointed to an office or position in Union shall be granted a leave of absence for a period of continuous service with Union. Fifteen (15) days' notice must be given the Company before the worker takes leave to accept such office or position or chooses to return to work. Such leave of absence shall be without pay. Seniority shall not be broken or suspended by reason of such leave.

B. A leave of absence without pay shall also be granted for temporary leave to conduct Union business provided reasonable notice is given.

SECTION XIV. *RIGHTS OF ACCESS TO COMPANY PROPERTY.*

A. Duly authorized and designated representatives of Union shall be permitted on Company premises in connection with the normal conduct of Union affairs.

B. In the exercise of the foregoing privilege, there shall be no unnecessary interference with the productive activities of the workers.

C. Before a Union representative contacts any of the workers during regular working hours, he shall notify Company that he is on the premises.

SECTION XV. *RECORDS AND PAY PERIOD.*

A. Company shall keep full and accurate records, including total hours worked, piece rate or incentive records, total wages and total deductions. Workers shall be furnished a copy of the itemized deductions each payday which shall include the worker piece rate production record.

B. Union shall have the right, upon reasonable notice given to Company, to examine time sheets, work production or other records that pertain to worker's compensation.

SECTION XVI. *BULLETIN BOARDS.*

Company will provide bulletin boards placed at such central locations as shall be mutually agreed, upon which Union may post notices.

SECTION XVII. *ROBERT F. KENNEDY FARMWORKERS MEDICAL PLAN.*

Effective as of the date of this Agreement, Company shall thereafter during the term of this Agreement contribute to the Robert F. Kennedy Farmworkers Medical Plan ten cents (10¢) per hour for each hour worked by all workers covered by this Agreement.

SECTION XVIII. *HEALTH AND SAFETY.*

Company and the United Farm Workers Organizing Committee, AFL-CIO recognize the need to protect and conserve human life, water, soil and vegetation. Economic poisons, when used incorrectly by a grower in agriculture on any crop, may be harmful to farm workers and to consumers, disrupt the earth's ecology and do not properly serve the farmers. In the hope of developing, with the help of Federal, State and University consultants, new, imaginative and creative approaches to the problem of conserving our natural resources, and in hope of taking progressive steps to protect the health of farm workers and consumers, Company and Union agree that the subject of economic poisons is a necessary and desirable subject for this collective bargaining agreement.

Company and Union agree as follows:

A. Union shall cause to be formed a Health and Safety Committee (the "Committee") comprised of workers' representatives. Members of the Committee shall have free access to all records concerning the use of economic poisons. The Committee shall participate in the formulation of rules and practices relating to the health and safety of workers including, but not limited to, the following: use of economic poisons; the use of garments, materials, tools and equipment as they may affect the health and safety of the workers; and sanitation conditions.

B. DDT, Aldrin, Dieldrin, Endrin, Parathion, TEPP and other economic poisons which are extremely dangerous to farm workers, consumers and the environment, shall not be used.

C. The Committee shall approve the use of organo-phosphates. Company will notify Committee at least seven (7) days prior to the application of organo-phosphate material. Such notice shall contain the information set forth in paragraph D, below. The Committee shall determine the length of time during which farm workers will not be permitted to enter a sprayed field following the application of an organo-phosphate pesticide. One baseline cholinesterase test and other additional tests shall be taken at the expense of Company when organo-phosphates are used. The results of said tests shall be given to Committee immediately, and, if requested, to an authorized Union representative.

D. The following records shall be kept and made available to the Committee and to any other authorized Union representative:

1. A plan showing the size and location of fields and a list of the crops or plants being grown.

2. Pesticides and economic poisons used including brand names plus active ingredients, registration number on the label and manufacturer's batch or lot number.

    (a) Dates and time applied or to be applied.

    (b) Location of crops or plants treated or to be treated.

(c) Amount of each application.

(d) Formula.

(e) Method of application.

(f) Person who applied the pesticide.

(g) Date of harvest.

E. No worker under this Agreement will be required to work when in good faith he believes that to do so would immediately endanger his health or safety.

F. There shall be adequate toilet facilities, separate for men and women in the field readily accessible to workers, that will be maintained in a clean and sanitary manner. These may be portable facilities and shall be maintained at the ratio of one for every forty workers or fraction thereof.

G. Each place where there is work being performed shall be provided with suitable, cool, potable drinking water convenient to workers. Individual paper drinking cups shall be provided.

H. Workers will have two (2) rest periods of ten (10) minutes which insofar as practical shall be in the middle of each work period.

I. Tools and equipment and protective garments necessary to perform the work and/or to safeguard the health of or to prevent injury to a worker's person shall be provided, maintained and paid for by Company, such as but not limited to: grape knives, rain gear, gloves, pruning shears, and umbrella for tractor drivers. Workers shall be responsible for returning all such equipment that was checked out to them, but shall not be responsible for breakage.

J. Adequate first aid supplies shall be provided and kept in clean and sanitary dust proof containers.

SECTION XIX. *GRIEVANCE PROCEDURES.*

A. The parties to the Agreement agree that for all differences, misunderstandings, or disputes which arise between Company and Union in regard to wages, working conditions or other conditions of employment, discharge or any other dispute, an earnest effort shall be made to settle any difference immediately as follows:

Step 1. Any disagreement or disputes between company and any worker, or union, shall be taken up within seven days of its discovery and the responding party shall respond immediately, if possible but no later than 24 hours from the presentation of the dispute and disagreement.

Step 2. In the event that such dispute cannot be settled within one work day, the matter shall be taken up by a Union representative with Company's representative.

Step 3. If the matter is not settled under Step 2 within two (2) work days, the matter in dispute shall be reduced to writing and submitted to Company's designated representative and a Union representative.

B. If the parties have not resolved a dispute arising out of the interpretation of this agreement within seven (7) working days, the matter shall be submitted to an arbitrator selected by Union and Company. If they cannot agree on an arbitrator, one will be chosen by the Federal Mediation and Conciliation Service, and his decision on the matter shall be final and binding on both parties.

C. A grievance committee of five (5) workers shall be established by the Union which committee may participate at any step of the grievance. If Company requests a meeting of this committee during working hours, Company shall pay the members for their time at their hourly rate or average piece rate.

D. Any disputes arising between Union and Company under Sections I, XXV, II or IV shall be taken up directly by Company's representative and Union's representative and shall proceed immediately to arbitration, if said persons cannot resolve the dispute within five (5) days.

E. All testimony taken at arbitration hearings shall be taken under oath, reported and transcribed. The arbitrator's fees and expenses shall be assessed as a part of his award against the losing party as he shall determine the same.

SECTION XX. *UNION LABEL.*

The parties contemplate that a Union label (certification mark) will enjoy a competitive advantage in the market. The parties wish to insure that the public cannot be deceived in purchasing non-union picked grapes under a fraudulent Union label (certification mark). In order to insure that such fraudulent marketing does not and cannot take place, the following information will be made available to an official representative of Union:

    A. *Labels or labelling process:*
        1. Name and registration number.
        2. Printing source.
        3. Amount ordered.
        4. Amount used.

    B. *Shipping information:*
        1. Method: truck, rail, air or sea.
        2. Name of shipper.
        3. Name of broker.
        4. Destination.
        5. Type of sales arrangements, including but not limited to district sales, consignments, credit, auction, contract or other arrangements.

    C. *Union Label or Seal.* Each lug and/or unit (as that term may be agreed upon) shipped shall bear the Union label or seal. The Union label or seal cannot be sold, transferred, or assigned in any manner. Company will place on each lug and/ or unit for sale in a visible manner a Union label such as the Union may designate.

    D. *Security Clause.* It is recognized that violation of this provision will cause actual damage which is difficult to ascertain, but which includes expenses attendant upon informing the consuming public of this misuse and misrepresentation of other non-union growers. These expenses will approximate $10,000. The damages for violation of this provision, therefore, shall be $10,000 plus $1,000 for each mislabeled carload shipped.

SECTION XXI. *MODIFICATION.*

No provision or term of this Agreement may be amended, modified, changed, altered or waived except by a written document executed by the parties hereto.

SECTION XXII. *DURATION.*

This Agreement shall be effective as of March 31, 1970. and shall continue through the 30th day of March, 1973. Thereafter, the Agreement shall continue in effect from year to year unless either party gives the other written notice of its intention to terminate, which notice shall be given sixty (60) days prior to any anniversary date of this Agreement. Notwithstanding the foregoing, either party shall have the right at any time after January 1 of a contract year to notify the other in writing of its desire to reopen Sections XVII, XVIII H and XXIII for the purpose of renegotiation, and if such renegotiation has not resulted in a mutual agreement prior to the end of said contract year, then the provisions of Section XXV shall become inoperative unless, on or before the end of said contract year the parties shall have mutually agreed to submit said issues to arbitration.

SECTION XXIII. *WAGES AND OTHER BENEFITS.*

A. Appendix A which is attached hereto and made a part hereof sets forth the schedule of wage rates which shall apply to all jobs in the bargaining unit.

B. Incentive and piece rate workers shall have guaranteed an hourly earnings rate of not less than the rate applicable to general labor as set forth in Appendix B of this Agreement.

C. A worker will be paid jury pay and/or witness pay for any days of work missed (not exceeding seven) due to the performance of such duty. Jury duty pay and/or witness pay is defined as the difference between the fees received by such worker for performing such duty and his regular earnings up to eight (8) hours per day for each such day of jury duty and/

or witness service. To receive pay under this provision, the worker must provide Company with a copy of notice summoning him to appear for jury duty or witness duty and if so requested, documentary evidence of the amount of jury fees and/or witness fees received for performing such duty.

D. Vacations with pay shall be granted to eligible workers who qualify for such vacations. Workers shall be eligible in the calendar year following the first anniversary of employment and annually thereafter for a two-week vacation, provided that, in order to qualify for vacation pay such worker must have worked two thousand (2,000) hours in the prior calendar year. Vacation pay will be computed on the basis of the hourly rate (or his average hourly piece rate earnings) applicable on the last day worked prior to the vacation.

E. Overtime pay based on time and a half shall be paid to all women and minors who work more than eight (8) hours per day.

SECTION XXIV. *HOURS OF WORK.*

A. A normal work day will consist of no more than eight (8) hours per day, Monday through Saturday. A normal work week will consist of forty-eight (48) hours.

B. The foregoing is not considered to be a guarantee of hours per day or hours per week.

SECTION XXV. *STRIKES, BOYCOTTS AND LOCKOUTS.*

A. There shall be no strikes, boycotts of union-picked grapes or lockouts.

B. If any of said events occur, the officers and representatives of Union and/or Company, as the case may be, shall do everything within their power to end or avert such activity.

SECTION XXVI. *COUNTERPARTS.*

This Agreement may be executed in counterparts, each of which when taken together shall constitute the original agreement between the parties.

IN WITNESS WHEREOF, the parties hereto have caused this Agreement to be executed as of the date and year first above written.

UNITED FARM WORKERS ORGANIZING COMMITTEE, AFL-CIO

By CESAR E. CHAVEZ

THE GRAPE AND FRUIT COMPANY

By LIONEL STEINBERG

Suggested Readings

ALLEN, STEVE. *The Ground Is Our Table*. New York: Doubleday, 1966.

DUNNE, JOHN GREGORY. *Delano*. New York: Farrar, Straus & Giroux, 1967.

FISHER, LLOYD. *The Harvest Labor Market in California*. Cambridge, Mass.: Harvard University Press, 1953.

GALARZA, ERNESTO. *Merchants of Labor*. Charlotte, Calif.: McNally & Loftin, 1964.

———. *Spiders in the House and Workers in the Field*. Notre Dame, Ind.: University of Notre Dame Press, 1970.

GREBLER, L.; MOORE, J. W.; and GUZMAN, R. C. *The Mexican-American People*. New York: The Free Press, 1970.

LONDON, JOAN; and ANDERSON, HENRY. *So Shall Ye Reap: The Story of Cesar Chavez and the Farm Workers' Movement*. New York: Crowell, 1971.

MCWILLIAMS, CAREY. *Brothers Under the Skin*. Boston: Little, Brown, 1939.

———. *Factories in the Field*. Boston: Little, Brown, 1939.

———. *Ill Fares the Land*. Boston: Little, Brown, 1942.

———. *North from Mexico*. Philadelphia: Lippincott, 1961 edition.

MATTHIESSEN, PETER. *Sal, Si Puedes*. New York: Random House, 1969.

NELSON, EUGENE. *Huelga!: The First Hundred Days of the Grape Strike*. Delano, Calif.: The Farm Worker Press, 1966.

PAZ, OCTAVIO. *The Labyrinth of Solitude: Life and Thought in Mexico*. New York: Grove Press, 1961.

U.S. Civil Rights Commission. *Mexican Americans and the Administration of Justice in the Southwest*. Washington, D.C.: Government Printing Office, 1970.